"WHAT I'D LIKE TO DO IS GO DOWN IN HISTORY AS THE PRESIDENT THAT MADE AMERICANS BELIEVE IN THEMSELVES AGAIN." —Ronald Reagan

"No president since Kennedy has had a voice at once so distinctive and beguiling…. It was the voice that carried him out of Dixon and away from the depression, the voice that more than any single attribute got him where he is." —Roger Rosenblatt of *Time* magazine, 1981

HIS VALUES "He was a star, a celebrity, a big shot—but he never acted that way. He didn't put on airs. He knew who he was and stayed that way all his life." —Lou Cannon, journalist and Reagan biographer

HIS VALUES "Most politicians talk about policies and the changing issues of the day. Ronald Reagan talked about principles—deeply held beliefs. The difference is profound. Policies shift with the breeze of public opinion, but principles are anchors, even in a storm."

—Jack Kemp, vice presidential nominee, cabinet secretary, and member of Congress

HIS VOICE "Not since Lincoln, or Winston Churchill in Britain, has there been a president who has so understood the power of words to uplift and inspire." —Margaret Thatcher, prime minister of Great Britain

HIS VISION "[He] was a man with a clear ideological vision, a man with a tough-minded view of the world, a man with a talent for devising unusual strategies to get what he wanted and a streak of rugged independence that was masked by the warmth of his personality."

—Martin Anderson, domestic and economic policy adviser, scholar, and author

"Reagan's greatness derives in large part from the fact that he was a visionary— a conceptualizer who was able to see the world differently from the way it was. While others were obsessed and bewildered by the problems of the present, Reagan was focused on the future." —Dinesh D'Souza, author, scholar, and Reagan biographer

RONALD REAGAN
AN AMERICAN HERO

★ *His Voice, His Values, His Vision* ★

A TEHABI BOOK

Ronald Reagan

PRESIDENTIAL FOUNDATION

WITH REFLECTIONS BY NANCY REAGAN
Introduction by William F. Buckley, Jr.

CONTENTS

For almost a half century it has been my pride and privilege to stand beside one of the most extraordinary men of our time. I've known his thoughts, shared his joys and triumphs, and felt his pain. Our path together has taken us to heights neither of us could have imagined, and through difficulties that, alone, neither of us might have endured. Through it all, the journey has truly been grand—for I have had the joy of traveling with my beloved companion, Ronald Reagan.

I've often said that when I married Ronnie, I thought I'd married an actor. Well, I quickly found that I'd married not just an actor but also a dynamic political leader! Before we knew it, we had left our peaceful lives in Hollywood to reside in the governor's mansion in Sacramento, and then, incredibly, in the White House, where Ronnie changed the world for the better and became one of the most beloved presidents of our time.

I should not have been so surprised by this turn of events—Ronnie's life has always been extraordinary. And as I flip through the pages of this book, I am overwhelmed by memories of his life and our life together: his humble Midwest beginnings; his sportscasting and acting careers; our years in public service as well

Reflections by Nancy Reagan

as our time spent among friends and family, saddled on horses at Rancho del Cielo, and relaxing at home. I also see old friends like Margaret Thatcher, Frank Sinatra, and (who would have thought it?) Mikhail Gorbachev, among many others. But mostly, I see Ronnie: the gifted world leader, the loving husband and father, a man of depth, humor, compassion, and love for his country, its people, and life itself.

Not all the memories are good. We faced an assassination attempt, several battles with cancer, the bleak days of Iran-Contra, now a long struggle with Alzheimer's—but Ronnie's unquenchable optimism and courage always saw him through, and buoyed me along as well. Part of his strength—and mine—came from you, the American people, to whom he dedicated his life of public service. Your letters, gifts, and prayers have encouraged and cheered us—and made us proud to live, as Ronnie would say, "in this great land we call America."

For your steadfast love and support, I thank you.

Nancy Reagan

NANCY REAGAN
February 6, 2001

This book is a work of devotional art. I am in the publishing business and happily record that I haven't seen a more beautiful biographical portrait of anyone, living or dead. The design is functional and ingenious, the text is, to be sure, worshipful—yet spare, and exquisitely presented on the page. The pictures are all of knock-em-dead quality, evoking episodes in the life of its subject, from schooldays—Schooldays? "There are advantages to being elected president. The day after I was elected, I had my high school grades classified as Top Secret"—through his myriad careers, right to retirement. And, at the very end, a single, small, candid photograph, capturing a kiss on his cheek on his eighty-nineth birthday by his wife, lover, nurse, and idol.

Contemplating this brief introduction after reading—and most important, viewing—the book, I have thought to say that whatever the skills of the editors, photographers, and designers who put it together, it could not have been assembled about anyone else. Just to begin with, there is the physical factor. An indulgent nature went extravagantly to work, endowing him and her with an extraordinary beauty. There is also the photogenic aptitude, matched perhaps by the two Kennedys, but otherwise unrivaled. Interrupt your reading of this text and turn to page 121,

A word from William F. Buckley, Jr.

a picture of the Reagans during the gubernatorial campaign. Turn then to page 182, the president toasting a foreign prime minister. Everything celebrated by this book is there in those pictures: grace, benignity, presence, pride.

If it sounds as if I have been carried away, that's how it should sound. Reagan's career is, like Lincoln's, mythologic from beginning to end. The son of unschooled parents and an alcoholic father brought up in Illinois farm country. A teenager who worked his way through college on an athletic scholarship. A college graduate looking for work during the depression, buoyed by the very idea of radio coverage of sports events, at which he excelled, even when the wires went dead, leaving him to imagine and relate what was going on in the stadium he couldn't see. On to Hollywood, then television, the Screen Actors Guild, the governorship, the White House, a historic democratic revalidation in 1984 and, soon after his retirement, the fruit of policies undertaken by him as president: the dissolution of a global threat, launched in 1917 when he was six years old, and the continued revival of the domestic economy.

Providence held out for Ronald Reagan. His mother had assured him, as a boy, that it would be so for a dutiful son. That was less than a divine assurance of uninterrupted good fortune. The pitfalls are here recorded, though they do not slow down the momentum of life and destiny fulfilled. The book does not make light of an assassination attempted, or a conclusive illness contracted. But the narrative adamantly reflects the character and temperament of the man it celebrates, the sunny and resourceful optimist. The reader is here to luxuriate in the heroic aspects of a life that lent itself to the making of historical poetry, and happily agrees to be edged into fantasy.

That life is captured by adroit text and recorded tributes from many of his countrymen; but, mostly, by pictures. These portray what journalist David Broder called "a kind of personal ease and charm that not only delighted his audiences, but disarmed his critics." The American whose "wit and grace he elevated to the level of legend."

This resplendent volume is fit celebration of that legend, this legend.

WILLIAM F. BUCKLEY, JR.
November 2000

An Emerging Voice

"My mother always told me that

His was a childhood of contrasts: Ronald Reagan was a golden youth in a time of national adversity, a time plagued by world war and economic disaster. Like many other Americans at the turn of the century, he was poor—but unfailingly happy and content. He was a church-going, hardworking, all-American kid—but one uniquely brushed by fate.

He was born on February 6, 1911, in an apartment above a bakery in the tiny hamlet of Tampico, Illinois. His father, John Edward Reagan—"Jack"—was a shoe salesman, an Irish Catholic whose ancestors had, like so many others, emigrated during Ireland's potato famine. His mother, Nelle Wilson Reagan, was of Scots-Irish descent, a mainstay of the Disciples of Christ church, a cheerful woman who believed in sharing her faith by living it. "While my father was a cynic and tended to suspect the worst of people, my mother was the opposite," her son would remember. "She always expected to find the best in people and often did, even among the prisoners at our local jail to whom she frequently brought hot meals."

When Ronald Wilson Reagan made his advent into the world, his father looked at him and prophetically, if facetiously, pronounced to his wife, Nelle: "He looks like a fat little Dutchman. But who knows, he might grow up to be president some day."

God has a plan for my life."

Thus, the boy became known as "Dutch." He liked his nickname, thinking it more rugged and manly than "Ronald."

On the surface, Nelle, Jack, Dutch, and his older brother, Neil (or "Moon" as his father had nicknamed him, after a comic-strip character), seemed a typical American family, but this was not quite true. Jack Reagan was, according to his younger son, "endowed with the gift of blarney and the charm of a leprechaun. No one . . . could tell a story better than he could." On his good days, Jack was indeed a bluff and bighearted charmer. But on his bad days, he suffered from what his sons came to call the "Irish disease": He drank himself into unconsciousness.

Even so, Jack had a restless ambition to improve himself, and during his sons' early years he shuttled the family around the Midwest as he pursued better jobs. When Dutch was nine, the Reagans finally settled in Dixon, Illinois, a modest, industry-driven town about ninety miles from Chicago. It was tiny at almost nine thousand people, but in Dutch's eyes, it was a large and grand place, with rich farmland that held untold adventure, and front porches that brimmed with country charm. "To me, it was heaven," Reagan would later remember. "It was a small universe where I learned standards and values that would guide me for the rest of my life."

It was in Dixon where he also began learning about his own special talents. In high school Dutch thrived, growing into a handsome, athletic six-footer who starred on the football team and, in his senior year, was elected student body president. Money was always scant in the Reagan family, but odd jobs and scholarships helped pay his way to Eureka College near Peoria, where he enrolled in 1928. His grades were just slightly above average—"My favorite subject was football," he liked to quip. Yet it was hardly for lack of intelligence; he had a photographic memory and had taught himself to read as a preschooler, later earning near-perfect marks as a first-grader. But in college he focused his energies on his real passions: athletics, campus politics . . . and acting. A standout in Eureka's drama club, he envisioned a future as a performer, on stage or in film, or perhaps on air as a sportscaster. Much as he loved the Midwest, he was drawn by promises beyond its flat horizon.

By the time Dutch Reagan left Eureka, the Great Depression had engulfed America like a black tidal wave. But with jaunty confidence and bedrock faith he followed his dream—to celebrity in the Midwest and greater fame in Hollywood, to California's governor's mansion, and finally to the great role he was destined to play, the presidency. America's heartland had shaped and defined the young Reagan; he would always carry it with him. But it had not set his limits.

HIS VALUES "I learned from my father the value of hard work and ambition, and maybe a little something about telling a story. From my mother, I learned the value of prayer, how to have dreams and believe I could make them come true.… I was raised to believe that God has a plan for everyone and that seemingly random twists of fate are all a part of His plan. My mother … told me that everything

in life happened for a purpose. She said all things were part of God's plan, even the most disheartening setbacks, and in the end, everything worked out for the best. If something went wrong, she said, you didn't let it get you down: You stepped away from it, stepped over it, and moved on." —Ronald Reagan

A 1913 Reagan family portrait taken in Tampico, Illinois, shows Jack, four-year-old Neil, two-year-old Ronald, and Nelle. Shortly after the picture was taken, the family moved to Chicago.

OUR BABY PICTURE

Ronald's baby picture, seen here in its original frame, was a prized part of the Reagan family gallery. By the time it was taken, the infant's father, Jack, had already dubbed him "Dutch."

"When I was a child, we moved a lot. My father was constantly searching for a better life and I was forever the new kid in school."

—Ronald Reagan

EARLY WANDERINGS

Perhaps because both were children of the pioneers who had settled America's prairies, Jack and Nelle Reagan had no trouble pulling up stakes to pursue opportunity.

With Dutch still a toddler, the family moved from Tampico, approximate population twelve hundred, to Chicago, a bustling city of crowds, gaslights, and horse-drawn carriages. The noisy hugeness of the place was wondrous, but the Reagans tasted only a small part; they lived in a cramped flat lit by a single gas jet that was encouraged to glow by depositing a quarter in a slot down the hall. Jack's salary from the Fair Store was so meager that even food was scarce, but Nelle made do. She could make one soup bone last for days, and on Sundays there was low-priced liver, bought from the butcher with the explanation that it was for the (entirely fictional) family cat.

Dutch was four when the family moved again, this time to Galesburg, west of Chicago. It was, Reagan remembered, "a completely different world. Instead of noisy streets and crowds of people, it consisted of meadows and caves, trees and streams, and the joys of small-town life." In the attic of their

The Reagans' first home in Dixon, at 816 South Hennepin Avenue, looks much the same today as it did when the family moved there in 1920. It was their first of five residences in Dixon.

rented house a previous tenant had left some collector's cases filled with birds' eggs and butterflies, and young Dutch spent enchanted hours with them whenever he could get time alone. He also looked forward to bedtime, when Nelle would station herself between him and his brother and read to them, tracing each line on the page with her finger. Following that maternal hand, Dutch learned to read as if through osmosis. His father, Jack, loved to tell how, one summer, he found his five-and-a-half-year-old son reading the Galesburg *Evening News*. None of the Reagans had realized Dutch knew how to read.

He entered the first grade in Galesburg, and the family was still there in 1917 when America entered World War I. By the time the war ended, the Reagans had moved again to another Illinois town, Monmouth. Shortly thereafter they came full circle, back to Tampico—but not for long. Jack, whose most cherished dream was to own his own shoe store, was about to receive at least a partial answer to his prayers: He earned a partnership in one. This move would end the Reagans' early wanderings and take them to Dixon, where Dutch's world would, at the same time, stabilize and change.

"Dutch was more quiet, retiring, he did more reading than his brother, Neil. I think he was very serious, more persistent about things he had to do." —Ed O'Malley, childhood friend and neighbor

Brick-paved Galena Avenue, with its drugstore, soda shop, and assortment of small businesses, was one of downtown Dixon's main streets in Dutch Reagan's day. The town's population at the time was around 9,000.

HIS VALUES *"He grew up in Dixon, Illinois, where life was wholesome, where people trusted each other, and nobody locked his door at night. People in Dixon stuck together and helped each other. To this day, Ronnie thinks that's the way it should be."* —Nancy Reagan

Dutch's early affinity for reading made him a regular at the Dixon Public Library, left, where he read books on wildlife and birds, college and football. The books about college life, he would later say, planted in him the first of many dreams of one day becoming a student.

First Street intersected with Galena, above, which ran toward the Memorial Arch. Along with its mercantile establishments, Dixon boasted a post office, shoe factory, cement plant, and several churches.

"Everyone has a place to come back to, and for me that place is Dixon." —Ronald Reagan

COMING HOME

Planted in farm country, Dixon was a picture-postcard town, a place where folks would no sooner have thought of locking their doors than of turning their backs on a neighbor in need. Dutch loved it.

"Almost everybody knew one another, and because they knew one another, they tended to care about each other," he would reminisce. "If a family down the street had a crisis—a death or serious illness—a neighbor brought them dinner that night. If a farmer lost his barn to a fire, his friends would pitch in and help him rebuild it." This sense of community and the deep faith that underlay it warmed him. He believed—he always would—in the power of prayer, and in Dixon he was baptized in Nelle's church, the Disciples of Christ.

Dutch would need his faith. Despite the town's charm, life there was no earthly paradise for him. He had long sensed something wrong in his family. "Sometimes, my father suddenly disappeared and didn't come home for days," he would remember, "and sometimes when he did return, my brother and I would hear some pretty fiery arguments through the walls of our house." Other times, Nelle would mysteriously bundle the boys off to visit relatives.

Nelle Reagan's serene smile mirrored her invincible optimism. This picture of her was taken during a visit to Dixon in 1951.

In Dixon, when they were old enough, she explained the mystery. "She said Jack [the Reagan boys always called their parents by their first names] had a sickness that he couldn't control—an addiction to alcohol," Reagan later recollected. Nelle told the boys they "shouldn't love him any less because [of it]. . . . If he ever embarrassed us, she said, we should remember how kind and loving he was when he wasn't affected by drink."

It was not easy. Jack's drinking was not constant—he might go a year or more without a drop—but a single drink would invariably lead to a bender, and the threat of one always loomed. One winter when Dutch was eleven, he came home and at his front door nearly stumbled over his father, passed out drunk. Mortified, he dragged Jack inside and put him to bed.

Guided by his mother, Dutch slowly made peace with Jack's problem. He clung to his love for his father and looked inward, and upward, for comfort. "I found a lot of enjoyment during those first years in Dixon in solitary ways," he would remember, "reading, studying wildlife, and exploring the local wilderness."

In the beauty of the woods, as in the quiet goodness of Dixon's townspeople, he found God, as surely as he found Him in church.

"My mother gave me a great deal, but nothing she gave me was more important than that special gift, the knowledge of the happiness and solace to be gained by talking to the Lord."

—Ronald Reagan, remarks on signing the 1987 National Day of Prayer Proclamation, December 22, 1986

"At church, you prayed side by side with your neighbors, and if things were going wrong for them, you prayed for them—and knew they'd pray for you if things went wrong for you." —Ronald Reagan

In his front yard in Dixon, twelve-year-old Dutch Reagan offers the camera a tentative smile. It was about this time that he had to drag his drunken father into the house.

TOLERANCE

Whatever his faults, Jack Reagan was fair-minded. And in his day, that was no mean achievement; prejudice in America was endemic.

It was a time when racial discrimination was legal in the South and a practical reality almost everywhere else, a time of excluding Jews from many public accommodations and private clubs, a time when black children and white children went to separate—and grossly unequal—schools, when signs hung over water fountains saying "Whites Only" or "Coloreds Only," and signs over stores said "No Dogs or Irishmen Allowed."

It was, perhaps, this last injustice that roused Jack's moral indignation and stirred him to instill in his sons a mind for tolerance.

During a business trip one winter, Jack checked into a hotel where a smirking clerk said, "You'll like it here, Mr. Reagan. We don't permit a Jew in the place."

"I'm a Catholic," Jack growled in reply. "If it's come to the point where you won't take Jews, then some day you won't take me either." With that, he picked up his suitcase and stalked out into a roaring blizzard, where—this being the only hotel in town—he slept in his car.

Nelle Reagan regarded bigotry as an assault on the

Jack and Ronald Reagan in the late 1930s, above. Shortly after arriving in Hollywood. Nelle Reagan poses with her handsome son, at left.

Golden Rule. "Treat thy neighbor as you would want your neighbor to treat you," she told her boys. She and Jack encouraged them to invite their black friends over and treat them no differently than their white playmates.

The boys took this to heart. Moon's best friend was African-American, and when they went to the movies, Moon sat with him in the balcony—the only place blacks were allowed.

Dutch, too, would stand against prejudice. In college, he encountered racism on a road trip to Dixon as he helped his coach register the team in a local hotel. "I can take everybody but your two colored boys," the clerk said. Appalled, Dutch suggested that the coach tell the team there was not enough room for everyone; he and the black players could stay at the Reagan house.

Given his upbringing, Reagan was both angry and dismayed when, decades later, political opponents from time to time called him "racist." During his first run for governor, he would, in fact, walk out on a debate when an opponent made an allegation of bigotry. Ordinarily, Reagan was uniquely resilient and forgiving in the face of criticism. But it seemed to him terribly unjust to be accused of one of the sins he most abhorred.

HIS VALUES "My parents constantly drummed into me the importance of judging people as individuals. There was no more grievous sin at my household than a racial slur or other evidence of religious or racial intolerance." —Ronald Reagan

THE FIRST PLATFORM

For the millions who came to admire him as a screen idol and then as a dynamic leader, it might be surprising to learn that Ronald Reagan was a classic late-bloomer sort of kid.

In grade school he was small and myopic, and as a result, dismal at most sports, languishing in the shadow of his bigger and more athletic older brother. When baseball teams formed on the playground, Dutch was always the last one chosen. "When I stood at the plate," he remembered, "the ball appeared out of nowhere." This severe nearsightedness fueled Dutch's love instead for football, a game in which, he later said, it didn't matter if his opponent's "face was blurred." All the fervor in the world, however, could not make up for his lack of physical strength. By the time he became a freshman at North Dixon High School, he was still only five feet, three inches tall and weighed a scrawny 108. He gamely battled to make the football team—and failed.

In his sophomore year, however, the adolescent began to sprout. Within a year he shot up to five feet, ten-and-a-half inches and a muscular 160, taking on the lean and square-jawed good looks that would later help fuel his movie career.

Lowell Park in Dixon was an idyllic setting for Dutch Reagan, adolescent lifeguard. It offered pretty scenery—and pretty girls.

He made the varsity football team, starting at right guard, and became a standout swimmer as well.

It was swimming, in fact, that led to what he called "one of the best jobs I ever had," one that would give him confidence and help fuel his metamorphosis from small boy to golden youth. After his sophomore year, and for seven consecutive summers, he was the lifeguard at Lowell Park. This wooded tract ran along the Rock River and was a popular gathering place for Dixonites.

Starting at fifteen dollars a week, Dutch worked at Lowell Park seven days a week, ten to twelve hours a day. The hours were long and the salary low, but money was hardly his only compensation. He had the satisfaction of saving seventy-seven people during his seven summers at the park. Perched high on his lifeguard's platform, looking tanned and handsome, he found his confidence building in the open admiration of the local girls.

One of those girls would become his first love. She was Margaret Cleaver, the pretty, dark-haired minister's daughter from Dutch's church. With a steady girl, some rewarding work, and a modicum of glory on the football field and the lifeguard's platform, Dutch Reagan's life was looking up.

"I kind of had to laugh at myself when I went to work at [Lowell Park] in the summers. You know why I had such fun at it? Because I was the only one up there on the guard stand. It was like a stage. Everybody had to look at me." —Ronald Reagan

"One of Dutch's tricks was to skip a pebble into the water, and when the startled swimmers looked around, he would say 'Oh, that's just an old river rat!' It was a trick designed to clear the area so he could leave work." —Ruth Graybill, operator of Lowell Park, in an interview in the *Dixon Telegraph*

Dutch, in the foreground, propels a canoe along the Rock River without benefit of a paddle. The lifeguard's job at Lowell Park helped him develop both his physique and his confidence.

A plaque memorializing Ronald Reagan's lifeguard days hangs in the Lowland Community House in Dixon. Oddly, one of the plaque's dates is wrong. Dutch began working at Lowell Park in 1926, not 1927.

"One of the proudest statistics of my life is seventy-seven— the number of people I saved during those seven summers."

—Ronald Reagan

"I remember one time when Dixon's most popular girl waved to me. At least I thought she was waving. My chest puffed out a little and I waved back. Then I turned away for a moment. When I looked again, she was going down. She had tried to signal for help." —Ronald Reagan

Dutch Reagan, above, standing in front of the Rock River at Lowell Park, in the early 1930s. Lowell Park's picnic grounds and unsullied waters, seen at left, made it the place to be for Dixonites during summer holidays. Crowds such as this usually made for a busy day for the young lifeguard.

"Dixon's only outdoor swimming facility was a treacherous place because of the unexpected undertow. There had been a series of drownings, and the Park Authority had considered closing Lowell Park to swimmers before Dutch undertook the job no one else wanted, an act Dixonites considered of extreme courage." —Anne Edwards, author and biographer

North Dixon Public Schools,
Dixon, Illinois.

PUBLIC SCHOOL 1868.

Dutch Reagan attended high school here at North Dixon High. It was here that he discovered he had both a talent and a taste for acting.

"I thought he was good. I knew he was different from most juveniles; he wanted to live the character. He didn't want to just parrot the lines; he gave a character feeling and dimension."

—B. J. Frazer, English teacher and head of the dramatics club, North Dixon High School

ON STAGE

Just as he seemed to inherit his mother's cheerful disposition, Ronald Reagan may also have derived from Nelle his love for dramatics. It is certain, in any case, that she gave him his first starring role.

In the small-town America of Dutch's day, movies were silent, traveling entertainers a rarity, radio still a novelty, and television not yet invented. So people had to entertain themselves and each other, and at this Nelle Reagan excelled. She starred in a group that gathered in homes and churches to recite bits of plays and poems, books, and speeches. "Nelle really threw herself into a part," Reagan would recall. "She loved it. Performing, I think, was her first love."

This being so, she tried to enlist her younger son—at the time still a bashful kid—to recite a speech at one of her gatherings. At first Dutch declined.

"My brother had already given several and had been a hit," he later explained. "But I was more shy and told my mother I didn't want to do it. Yet I guess there was something competitive enough in me that made me want to try to do as well as my brother and I finally agreed."

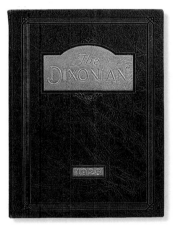

"I wonder what it's all about, and why/We suffer so, when little things go wrong?/We make our life a struggle/When life should be a song."

An optimist already, young Reagan penned this poem for his high school yearbook.

Nelle helped him memorize the speech, and it was a success. "I didn't know it then," Reagan said, "but, in a way, when I walked off the stage that night, my life had changed."

It would change again in high school. About the same time that Lowell Park and Margaret Cleaver entered Dutch's life, so did a new English teacher at North Dixon High. His name was B. J. Frazer, and he emphasized creativity over rote learning. Frazer encouraged Dutch to write imaginative essays, then to read them in class. His writings were, to his relief, met with laughter and approval. He later recalled, "The reaction of my classmates was more music to my ears."

Dutch had found the magic of an audience. "I tried out for a student play directed by Frazer—and then another," he remembered. "By the time I was a senior, I was so addicted to student theatrical productions that you couldn't keep me out of them."

In pretending to be other people, Dutch had found his release—and his true self. The stage made him more confident, more outgoing, and these qualities drew people to him. He capped his high school triumphs with his election as president of the student body. His star had begun to shine.

HIS VOICE "I had Ronald Reagan in school. He was so good in plays. He had an excellent voice. I think Ronald learned a lot from his mother, she had an excellent voice. We were proud of him. We used to say, 'Don't miss that play, Ronald Reagan is in it.' " —Geraldine Ryan, North Dixon High School teacher

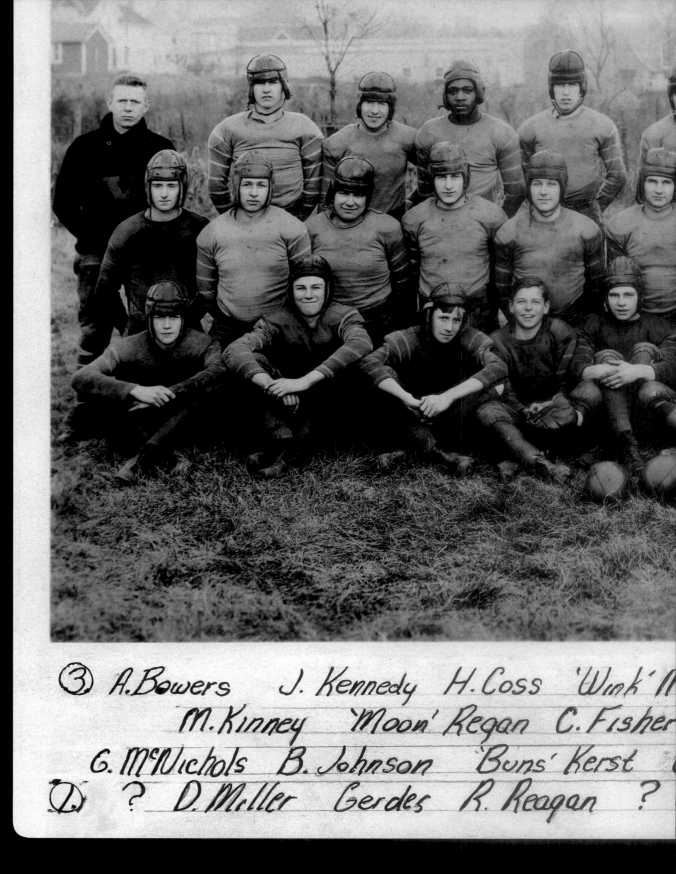

Dutch Reagan's yearbook picture, above top, in his senior year at North Dixon High, shows a rather solemn young man. He looks more at ease in the football squad photo, above, from the same yearbook.

③ A.Bowers   J. Kennedy H.Coss 'Wink' II

M.Kinney 'Moon' Regan C.Fisher

G. McNichols B. Johnson 'Buns' Kerst

⑩ ? D. Miller Gerdes R. Reagan ?

"He was like a big brother to me. I patterned my youth, kind of, after him. He was the perfect specimen of an athlete, tall, willowy, muscular, brown, good-looking. Of course, the girls were always flocking around him." —Bill Thompson, childhood friend

old's G. O'Malley C. Keyes R. McNichols
Culley ② M. Keller F. Kellar L. Miller
nde H. Weinman Wilson H. Marks E. Beach
uson ? ? K. Segner J. Padgett ? F. Spotts

E. C. Smith School, above top, provided Dutch's elementary-school education after the Reagans moved to Dixon in 1920. He finished the fifth grade here before moving on to South Central Elementary School.

Dixon's South Central Elementary and High School, above, saw Dutch through the sixth grade. When the family moved to the north side of the Rock River in 1922, he attended the North Grade School and then North Dixon High School.

NORTH DIXON HIGH

Both Dutch Reagan (first row, fourth from left) and his brother, nicknamed Moon (third row, third from right), appear in this photo of the 1927-28 North Dixon High football team. The team went 2-5 on the season, but classmates remember that Dutch was a strong addition at tackle. Like many players in his day, the young Reagan played defense as well.

"When Reagan played football for North Dixon High, the *Telegraph* reported that he had missed the extra point attempt after a touchdown. Fifty-five years after that game, Reagan told me it wasn't him but someone else who had missed that point. He loved football so much that the memory had remained in his consciousness. We printed a correction the next day."

Movie star Ronald Reagan endures some friendly swats from his TKE frat brothers during a 1941 trip to his alma mater. Success and celebrity never dimmed his love for his old school; he visited Eureka College at least a dozen times after graduating in 1932.

"In later life, I visited some of the most famous universities in the world. As governor of California, I presided over a university system regarded as one of the best. But if I had to do it over again, I'd go back to Eureka or another small college like it in a second." —Ronald Reagan

EUREKA!

A college education was hardly a tradition in the Reagan family. Like many working-class people in turn-of-the-century America, neither Jack nor Nelle had finished grade school. Fewer than 7 percent of Americans went to college. But Dutch was determined to be one of them.

It cannot be said that he yearned for academic glory; what he loved was the idea of college life and college football. He also loved Margaret Cleaver, who was planning to attend Eureka College, a small liberal arts school southeast of Dixon, owned by the Disciples of Christ church. (He and Margaret would date throughout college. Career paths would separate them, however, and in time Margaret would marry someone else.)

Dutch had managed to save four hundred dollars toward college, but it was not enough. When he drove Margaret to Eureka to enroll, therefore, he corralled the college president and the football coach and talked them into a scholarship to cover half his tuition. The rest he managed with his savings and a job washing dishes.

Dutch cut a dashing figure on campus. He had grown to six feet one and 175 pounds. Coeds were enchanted by his lopsided smile and courtly manners, and the boys admired his athleticism and affability. When Eureka's administration mandated fiscal cuts that would have prevented upperclassmen from graduating, it was Dutch who, only a freshman, led a successful strike in protest. It was his first political speech and a heady triumph. "For the first time in my life," he would recollect, "I felt my words reach out and grab an audience, and it was exhilarating."

He also stood out on the gridiron, making the varsity team in his sophomore year, but he was less impressive in the classroom. With his phenomenal memory, he easily maintained the C average he needed to be eligible for sports, and he did not strive for better; he believed there was more to education than academics. He preferred to explore his interests through extracurricular activities.

By his senior year, he had spent—along with his exploits in sports—two years as yearbook features editor, two in the student senate, three as president of the Eureka Boosters Club, and one as captain and coach of the swim team and student body president.

"If I had gone to one of those larger schools, I think I would have fallen back in the crowd and never discovered things about myself that I did at Eureka," he later assessed. "My life would have been different."

Reagan's athletic letter sweater from Eureka now resides in the Ronald Reagan Presidential Library.

"He would take a book the night before the test and in about a quick hour he would thumb through it and [mentally] photograph those pages and write a good test."

—"Moon" Reagan, recounting his brother's photographic memory

The Prism was Eureka's yearbook, and Dutch was the features editor of its 1932 edition. His writing talent was not inconsiderable, as his speechwriters would observe many years later.

"Everything good that has happened to me— everything— started here on this campus."

—Ronald Reagan

Taylor   Alcorn   Cottrell   Houghton   Reagan

THE PRISM

Well, folks! Here we are! and we've had a gay old time putting out the 1932 Prism! What? Sarcasm? No, why? Oh, I see! Well, of course, there were a few things. Sometimes, for instance, we hated to meet the editor on the campus after he had already asked three or four times for copy due! And then, we guess the business management had some little trouble scraping together ideas to paint the financial side of the canvas, (don't suppose you have forgotten that thrilling basketball opener between the Faculty and the town men!) Sometimes we had to hurry to make our discounts, and sometimes it rained and the photographer had to come back another day! But, after all the trouble and worry, it's really been a pleasurable undertaking, and we know a worthy one.

This year we have something new in the style of our division pages, a combination of ideas, modern and different. Our page borders are something different than anything used in any of the preceding Prisms. The organization of the opening section has been somewhat changed from last year's Prism. This year we have also included pictures of the advisers of the three upper classes, along with the class pictures and write-ups. We so well liked the honor Senior division introduced in last year's book, that we have decided to continue it, and hope that succeeding editors will not drop it from their books.

We would here like to ask those students, who have advertised in this book, to come in the office and pay for their ads before Christmas of next year; the Prism is in dire necessity of cash to pay for its patent rights.

Page One Hundred Twenty-four

"As in a small town, you couldn't remain anonymous at a small college. Everybody was needed. Whether it's the glee club or helping to edit the school yearbook, there is a job for everyone, and everybody gets a chance to shine at something and build their self-confidence." —Ronald Reagan

Radebaugh   Masocco   McCallister   Butchart   Muller

This year's staff would not stoop so low as to print satire in an otherwise perfectly good book, so we have decided to publish that old masterpiece which you will find back there among the ads, entitled "With Hamilton in Eureka, or Doomed by the Mill Race". The author of this elaborately penned treasure will be furnished upon receipt of your name, ten cents, and a self-addressed stamped envelope.

Seriously . . . we wish to thank everyone not mentioned in the staff, who has written copy, or helped the staff in any way in editing the 1932 Prism.

STAFF

KANARDY L. TAYLOR	Editor-in-chief
CHAPMAN COTTRELL	Business Manager
WILFRED MULLER	Asst. Bus. Mgr. and Circulation
RAYMOND MCCALLISTER	Athletics
TRESSIE MASOCCO	Women's Athletics
RUTH BUTCHART	Activities
WALTER RADEBAUGH	Seniors
MARJORIE ALCORN	Juniors
BERNICE HOUGHTON	Snapshots
RONALD REAGAN	Features

Solicitors—ELIZABETH BRUBAKER, MARY MCGUIRE, DOROTHY DOAN, DEAN BRADLE.

Moon Reagan attended Eureka at the same time as his younger brother, although he enrolled later. In their boyhood days, Moon had been so good at singing, dancing, and reciting that it seemed to some that he might turn out to be the actor in the family.

Ronald Reagan's Eureka class ring is on display at the Ronald Reagan Presidential Library.

HIS VOICE "He used to take an old broom from the locker room and pretend it was a microphone and 'announce' the game play by play afterwards. Never forgot a play either! He understood football—and baseball for that matter, too, better than most of the teams combined." —Mac McKinzie, Eureka College football and swim coach

LINE FOR
1¢ RESTAURANT
20 MEALS FOR $1.
DONATIONS INVITED
HELP FEED THE HUNGRY
1¢ WILL FEED 20
1¢ RESTAURANT
107 W. 43rd ST.

A long line of unemployed people wait to be fed in New York City in February 1932. FDR had not yet taken office, and without government relief programs, free food had to be distributed with private funds.

"In Dixon, troubles in the farming economy had begun months before the crash and when the full force of the depression struck, it hit our town like a cyclone." —Ronald Reagan

HARD TIMES

When the stock market crashed in October 1929, Ronald Reagan was in his sophomore year at Eureka. An eighteen-year-old sheltered in the womblike warmth of college life, he could scarcely have imagined the horror to come. In fact, few who lived before or long after the Great Depression could have imagined it either: America's economy in shambles; millions unemployed; mothers unable to feed their children; fathers leaving home to roam the country in desperate search of work, standing in breadlines, forced into the dreary havens of soup kitchens whose charity flayed their pride even as it fueled their bodies.

In a way, the Reagans escaped the worst of it: They lost nothing in the crash—the dubious advantage of having nothing much to lose. But there was enough despair and heartbreak to go around in those days, and they got their share. When it began, Jack was part owner of a nice shoe store, his share paid for by his labor. But as the lights on Dixon's main street winked out in the dark of the Great Depression, the store was among the casualties. Nelle supported the family for a time by working in a dress shop. Jack looked for a job, finally becoming a traveling shoe salesman working on commission.

Millions of Americans, desperate for hope and reassurance, gathered around radios such as the one pictured above to hear FDR's Fireside Chats.

One Christmas Eve when the boys were home from school, Jack got a special-delivery letter. He was expecting a Christmas bonus, and the family watched, waiting for good news, as he opened the envelope and read its contents.

"Well, that's a hell of a Christmas present," he told them. "I've been laid off." Soon thereafter, Nelle had to call Dutch at college and ask to borrow fifty dollars of his savings to pay the grocery bill. He was glad to give it, but both mother and son were shamed for Jack. They kept the loan a secret, shielding him from this worst indignity.

There was hope on the horizon, though. In 1932 Franklin Delano Roosevelt was elected president. With him came his New Deal: huge, prime-the-pump federal spending for relief programs and for vast public works projects aimed at creating jobs. Jack was a New Deal Democrat to his core, and Dutch, now old enough to vote for the first time, had also cast an enthusiastic ballot for FDR. Jack got a job administering a federal relief program in Dixon (and, on his own time, trying to find his clients work), and Dutch got a close look at government in action.

He knew the New Deal was necessary given the times and he applauded FDR's efforts. Yet it bothered Dutch to

"I was twenty-one and looking for work in 1932, one of the worst years of the Great Depression. And I can remember one bleak night in the thirties when my father learned on Christmas Eve that he'd lost his job. To be young in my generation was to feel that your future had been mortgaged out from under you." —Ronald Reagan

watch the lumbering bureaucracy and see how government handouts destroyed dignity and sapped initiative—and his political thinking would change in coming years as a result. Even as he came to despise the cumbersome "welfarism" the New Deal had spawned, however, he never lost his admiration for its creator.

"He'd entered the White House facing a national emergency as grim as any the country has ever faced," Reagan said of Roosevelt, "and, acting quickly, he had implemented a plan of action to deal with the crisis." He conceded that "FDR in many ways set in motion the forces that later sought to create big government and bring a form of veiled socialism to America"—but inadvertently: The measures he instituted as emergency stopgaps took on a life of their own and got out of hand.

Reagan would point out that FDR had run "on a platform dedicated to reducing waste and fat in government. He called for cutting federal spending by 25 percent, eliminating useless boards and commissions and returning to states and communities powers that had been wrongfully seized by the

federal government. If he had not been distracted by war, I think he would have resisted the relentless expansion of the federal government that followed him."

Whatever the New Deal's faults, young Dutch Reagan, like millions of others, was caught up in the magic of Roosevelt himself, that distinctive voice on the radio that soothed him and spoke directly to America in the famous Fireside Chats. Reagan would remember how FDR's "strong, gentle, confident voice resonated across the nation with an eloquence that brought comfort and resilience to a nation caught up in a storm and reassured us that we could lick any problem."

It was from Franklin Roosevelt that Reagan learned much about the very essence and style of the presidency, the firmness of purpose, the dignity tempered by warmth. One day it would stand him in good stead. But in the depths of the Great Depression, that day was as yet undreamed of. Dutch Reagan was just a young man who had faced harsh realities but still dreamed big dreams, who must now set out to make them reality.

ECONOMIC OPPORTUNITY

★

The Great Depression would dramatically shape Dutch's economic views. As he witnessed millions of Americans forced to accept government handouts, his belief in economic opportunity intensified. All people, he believed, should be able to work hard and prosper, to pursue the American dream. Later he said in his first inaugural address: "Government can and must provide opportunity, not smother it; foster productivity, not stifle it. This Administration's objective will be a healthy, vigorous, growing economy."

"FDR was one of the most influential figures in Ronnie's life. His New Deal brought hope and relief to the Reagans, and Ronnie never forgot that. In fact, he memorized FDR's 1933 inaugural address and used to quote it at length." —Nancy Reagan

HIS VOICE "He came to political maturity during the FDR era, having listened intently to the Fireside Chats on the radio. He not only memorized some of Roosevelt's passages but he also learned that to reach people effectively in their living rooms, a leader should speak with directness, simplicity and warmth." —David R. Gergen of *U.S. News and World Report*

Franklin Delano Roosevelt was a master at using the new medium of radio to keep in touch with the nation. A towering presence who saw America through the Great Depression and World War II, Roosevelt had young Ronald Reagan's unalloyed admiration.

Dutch (kneeling, fifth from left) served as president of the North Dixon High Dramatics Club during the 1928-29 school year. His mentor, B. J. Frazer, is at the right end of the lower row.

HIS VALUES "He wasn't the best student I had. But the one thing that set Dutch apart from all the others was that he never compromised his potential. Once he achieved a certain level of success, he would seek

but a new, greater challenge rather than sit back and enjoy it. He did that throughout his life. That was his secret. It was how he rose above the rest."

—B. J. Frazer, English teacher and head of the Dramatics Club, North Dixon High School

An Aspiring Voice

"There are worse things to

Of all the gifts Nelle Reagan passed on to her younger son, her optimism was no doubt the greatest. And her lesson that Dutch most took to heart was that God has a plan, that things work out in the end, and that even setbacks, viewed aright, are merely doorways to greater opportunities. Believing this, Ronald Reagan seemed always to trust, even during hard times, that fortune was about to smile. And almost invariably it did, bringing within his reach dreams that had once seemed as distant as the stars.

During the Great Depression, a job—of any kind—was beyond the grasp of many, and to aspire to so glamorous a pinnacle as a movie or stage career seemed a little unrealistic even to Dutch. But he did have a fallback plan to achieve celebrity on a slightly less exalted scale: He wanted to be a radio sports announcer.

Through a series of circumstances that in retrospect would seem nearly miraculous, a sports announcer he became. The job would be not only a pleasant interlude in itself—"If I had stopped there," he once remarked, "I believe I would have been happy for the rest of my life"—but it would also be a springboard toward future security, for himself and his whole family.

A trip to California would lead to a fortuitous meeting with an old friend, and from there to a talent agent, and suddenly Dutch would find himself under contract to a major movie studio. Made over for Hollywood, with a new look and a new

be called than a dreamer."

name (his own, as it turned out), Ronald Reagan seemed poised for stardom. Then the serial serendipity seemed to end, as he discovered anew what he had learned in his football days: Making the team was not the same as making the first string.

He languished in low-budget quickie films for a time, becoming, as he put it, "the Errol Flynn of the B pictures." But then came a breakout role: As the collegiate gridiron great George Gipp in *Knute Rockne—All American*, Reagan made moviegoers weep and producers take notice. Then came *Kings Row*, which boosted him toward A-movie status.

Yet the same year that *Kings Row* was released—in 1942—World War II was raging and Reagan was called to serve at Fort Mason, near San Francisco. By 1945 the war was over, but his Hollywood career had lost momentum. Though he made almost half of his fifty-three films after World War II, Reagan's absence in the industry would cost him.

His star was rising, however, in other areas. Reagan became active in the Screen Actors Guild and was eventually elected SAG's long-term president. As such, he became an excellent negotiator, which would yield rich benefits for his fellow actors and stand him in good stead later in life on a much wider stage. Under his leadership, SAG won its members studio-funded pension plans and medical plans and, toward the end of Reagan's tenure, earned them "residuals"—fees paid for actors' work on television reruns. His union activities would have other far-reaching consequences. Just as Reagan's early political thinking had been shaped by FDR and the New Deal, so would his changing views be molded by his confrontation with communism during the divisive, difficult days of that ideology's attempt to infiltrate the American film industry.

Lest Ronald Reagan ever doubt that a divine plan was at work, SAG also led him to what he would come to regard as the most phenomenal bit of luck in all his long and lucky life: On a mission to help a young actress named Nancy Davis, he found his one great and abiding love, the perfect companion for the path he would one day travel.

That love had come to him when he most needed it. Shortly thereafter, his career would reach another crossroads: In the 1950s, Hollywood's powerful studio system was disintegrating, partly due to the arrival of television. Many stars could only watch as their careers declined and guttered out. But Reagan was able to make a graceful leap from large screen to small. As host and sometimes star of television's *General Electric Theater,* he would find a new career that would also reveal promising vistas beyond acting. Once again, what looked like a stumbling block had turned out to be a paving stone. Of course, Nelle Reagan could have told him as much.

HIS VISION "When he graduated from Eureka College during the depths of the depression, he had no prospects of a job. But the world was one vast opportunity for Ronald Wilson Reagan. He had faith in the future of the country and in his own future, and his unfailing

HOLLYWOODLAND

optimism and self-deprecating humor commended him to others....
He succeeded at everything that he tried." —Lou Cannon, journalist and Reagan biographer

The "Hollywoodland" sign was built in 1927 by a real estate company. Though the firm went bankrupt during the depression, the sign became a landmark. In 1949 the "land" was removed during a renovation.

HIS VALUES "I started out hitchhiking, with only a few dollars in my pocket, trying station after station, usually failing to mention that I wanted to be a sports announcer—just simply saying I would

DUTCH'S BIG BREAK

America owes much to Montgomery Ward: Had the store hired Dutch Reagan, he might never have left Illinois. In fact, though, it did not, and at the time he was heartbroken.

Fresh out of college, Dutch had spent the last of his savings traveling to Chicago in search of a radio announcer's job, only to be met with closed doors. It was, after all, a time when 26 percent of America's workforce was unemployed. He hitchhiked home to find that Montgomery Ward was opening a store in Dixon, and a job was available managing the sporting goods department for $12.50 a week. He jumped at the prospect of steady employment—and fell flat. The job was offered to one of his Dixon classmates.

Broke, Reagan recalled some advice from his futile trip to Chicago: Try for an announcer's job in the sticks, at a small station where he could get experience and work his way up. With nothing but hope and the loan of his family's car, he set out for the Iowa-Illinois border, where a smattering of the nation's few commercial radio stations lay.

At WOC in Davenport, Iowa, he got some bad news from the program director, a Scotsman named Peter

A replica of the WHO microphone Reagan used is on display at the Ronald Reagan Presidential Library.

MacArthur. Dutch was a day late; an announcer's slot had just been filled. Crestfallen, he walked toward the elevator, muttering, "How the hell can you get to be a sports announcer if you can't even get a job at a radio station?"

"Hold on, you big bastard," MacArthur's burr rang out. "What was that you said about *sports* announcing?"

The upshot was an audition in which Dutch narrated with gusto the last quarter of a victorious Eureka game. MacArthur was impressed. For five dollars and bus fare, he offered, Dutch could broadcast an upcoming Iowa-Minnesota game. Reagan did well enough to announce three more games, but then the season ended and so did his job.

He spent the winter of 1932-33 unemployed, but the spring brought a fateful call from MacArthur: A staff announcer's job at WOC was available at one hundred dollars a month. Dutch was there the next day.

It was a rocky start. Dutch was not a sports announcer but a disc jockey, and he was not very good at it. He was almost fired before fate intervened with a chance to broadcast the Drake Relays, one of the nation's biggest track meets, for sister station WHO in Des Moines. He did so well that

like to get into the announcing part of the trade—I figured sports announcing was a higher ambition that would come later—but telling that I would do anything, take any job, to get started." —Ronald Reagan

WHO offered him the perfect job: sportscasting.

With fifty thousand watts' worth of his warm and resonant voice wafting across the Midwest, Dutch was soon a regional celebrity. His now seventy-five-dollar-a-week salary plus fees from speaking engagements enabled him to send money home—a godsend since Jack, now suffering from heart trouble, was unable to work. Dutch's good fortune was also a springboard for his brother. During a visit to Des Moines, Moon got into some on-air byplay with Dutch, matching predictions on the results of upcoming football games. It caught on with the public, leading to a regular show and launching Moon's ascent from announcer to program director and later to director, producer, network executive, and at last vice president of a top advertising agency.

Dutch loved his own work; he simply loved radio. "Radio was magic," he would reminisce. "It was theater of the mind. It forced you to use your imagination." And he found on one occasion that imagination was all he had.

In those days, many sportscasters reported games not by

A 1934 WHO postcard shows Reagan with his two favorite props: his mike and his pipe. The Irish setter at his feet was named Peggy after his childhood sweetheart, Margaret Cleaver.

being there, but by embroidering on information that ticked into their newsrooms across a telegraph wire. Dutch was a master at this, and one of his favorite memories was of a baseball game that tested his talent to the limit. In a scoreless tie, St. Louis and Chicago were in the ninth inning, with Dizzy Dean on the mound for the Cardinals and Billy Jurges at bat for the Cubs. Dutch had Dean's pitch en route to the plate when he read a note: "The wire's gone dead."

What to do with that pitch? Improvising in the breach, Dutch had Jurges foul it off. Then he described how kids in the stands were fighting for the ball. He prayed for the wire to start. It did not. Desperately, he announced that Jurges had hit another foul. And another. And another. On it went for almost seven endless minutes. Then his operator handed him a note that told the awful truth. The wire had started up again. Its message: "Jurges popped out on the first ball pitched."

Dutch sheepishly kept that bit of news to himself, leaving his many fans in the Midwest to wonder whether, with that awesome barrage of fouls, Billy Jurges had set some kind of record.

"I've often wondered at how lives are shaped by what seem like small and inconsequential events, how an apparently random turn in the road can lead you a long way from where you intended

to go. For me, the first of these turns occurred in the summer of 1932, in the abyss of the depression." —Ronald Reagan

Sportscasting at Des Moines radio station WHO made Reagan a local celebrity throughout the Midwest in the mid-1930s. His program's sponsor was a tobacco company, which explains the pipe.

All the members of the 1934 Chicago Cubs signed the team picture for Reagan, who broadcast their games that year. Three years later, his association with the Cubs would take him to Hollywood.

HIS VOICE "I think that was a very good training ground for him.... Because if you look at where Reagan is really a master communicator, it is on radio." —Lou Cannon, journalist and Reagan biographer

Fab Rawalis
Joe Yitter Chuck Klein
Bill Jurges Tuck Stainback
Bryant Augie Galan Tex Carleton
Clyde Shoun Frank Demaree
Hugh Casey Van Mungo
Gabby Hartnett

Before he'd mastered his communication skills, Dutch almost lost his first radio job at WOC. His slot was given to a teacher, who he was ordered to train. Midway through the training session, however, Dutch's replacement heard about his sudden firing and demanded a contract from WOC. The station refused, so the teacher quit—and while managers looked for another announcer, Dutch honed his on-air skills. Soon, WOC stopped talking about replacing Reagan, and he had locked in his dream job.

"At twenty-two I'd achieved my dream: I was a sports announcer. If I had stopped there, I believe I would have been happy the rest of my life. I'd accomplished my goal and enjoyed every minute of it." —Ronald Reagan

Ronald Reagan shows off the good effects of his studio makeover at the Chinese Theater on Hollywood Boulevard. Next to him is studio head Jack Warner and Sid Grauman, then-owner of the famed theater.

"They circled around me as if I were a racehorse. They spoke only to each other, not to me. I recall their saying such clinical things as 'What are we going to do with him?'" —Ronald Reagan

WELCOME TO CALIFORNIA

Though happy as a sports announcer, Dutch Reagan had never quite abandoned his greater dream of becoming an actor. It was there in 1937 when he arranged to have WHO pay his expenses to cover the Chicago Cubs' summer training camp on the California island of Catalina. Catalina was very close to Hollywood.

During his trip, he had dinner with a former colleague at WHO, a young singer named Joy Hodges, and to her he confided his yen to act.

"Take off your glasses," she said. He did, and his boyish good looks shone full force.

Joy arranged for him to meet the next day with an agent, Bill Meiklejohn, and it was to this nearly invisible personage—thanks to Joy, the glasses were still off—that Dutch gave a wildly inflated account of his theatrical experience. He ended with the crucial question: Could he realistically make it in Hollywood?

Without reply, Meiklejohn phoned Max Arnow, a casting director for Warner Brothers. "Max," he said, "I have another Robert Taylor sitting in my office."

"God made only one Robert Taylor," said Arnow, but he agreed to have a look. Arnow met with Dutch and, liking what he saw, arranged a screen test. He would show

Warner Brothers promoted its newcomer as the all-American good guy—an obvious piece of typecasting.

it to studio head Jack Warner, Arnow said, and get back to Dutch in a few days. Dutch coolly replied that he was leaving tomorrow for Des Moines. And he did, cursing himself cross-country for not staying.

But two days after he arrived home, a telegram came: "WARNERS OFFERS CONTRACT SEVEN YEARS STOP ONE YEAR OPTION STOP STARTING $200 A WEEK STOP WHAT SHALL I DO MEIKLEJOHN."

He sped to the Western Union station and replied: "SIGN BEFORE THEY CHANGE THEIR MINDS." A month later he threw everything he owned into his Nash convertible and headed for Hollywood.

Once there, however, the studio quickly dismantled his look, informing him of his many flaws: His clothes were a mess; his hair a disaster; his neck too short; and his head too small in proportion to his shoulders, which were too wide, and his chest, which was too broad.

A new hairdo and some artful tailoring took care of most of it, but there remained the problem of his name. Dutch Reagan was all wrong for a marquee.

"How about Ronald?" he ventured. "Ronald Reagan?"

Max Arnow and some Warners press agents kicked it around. Not bad, they decided. It would do.

"When I was announcing sports I was happy and thought that was all I wanted out of life. Then came the chance at Hollywood and that was even better." —Ronald Reagan

THE NATURAL

Sometimes it took months for a new contract player to get his first role. But it was only a matter of days before Ronald Reagan, shaking with stage fright, found himself before the cameras for the first time. Fortunately, the outing wasn't much of a stretch: The movie was called *Love Is on the Air*, and he played a radio announcer.

The film earned him some nice reviews. The *Hollywood Reporter*, one of the industry's most respected trade journals, called him "a natural." But his first movie also set a pattern: Reagan worked steadily in a series of frothy, forgettable B pictures, playing a handsome, all-American good guy in one incarnation or another. "I usually played a jet-propelled newspaperman who solved more crimes than a polygraph machine," he said. "My one unvarying line, which I always snapped into a telephone, was: 'Give me the city desk. I've got a story that will crack this town wide open.'"

It was not exactly Shakespeare but the money was good, and Warners, which had the option of canceling his contract after the first six months, kept him on. Secure, Reagan brought his parents to California and settled

Snapshots show the private side of movie actor Ronald Reagan. In the center he coaxes daughter Maureen into the swimming pool.

them in an apartment, then in a home of their own, ending forever the financial worries that had always plagued them.

He was pleased and proud to be able to do it, and Jack and Nelle loved their new life.

Reagan also started a new family during his early days in Hollywood. In 1940 he began an eight-year marriage to actress Jane Wyman. They had a daughter, Maureen, and adopted a son, Michael, before the marriage ended in divorce.

As the decade began, Ronald Reagan was investing most of his energy in the frustrating struggle to move from B pictures to A. But events in the wider world were converging in a global conflagration that would, for a time, dwarf and engulf all personal ambitions. On December 7, 1941, planes of the Empire of Japan mounted a sneak bombing attack on the American naval base at Pearl Harbor, Hawaii, and the United States entered World War II. Too myopic for combat, Reagan, a reserve officer, saw active duty making training films for the Army Air Corps. He entered as a second lieutenant and emerged four years later as a captain.

When he returned to his career, he found the movie industry in a state of flux. America had won the war, but Hollywood was undergoing upheavals of its own.

HIS VALUES "He would make suggestions as many actors do, but what I found with Ronnie is that the suggestions were helpful and not particularly self-serving. He was willing to give up a line not to help himself but to make the scene play better." —Fred De Cordova, director of *Bedtime for Bonzo*

"[Ordinary Americans] can see in Reagan a reflection of life as it ought to be—the boy from a middling poor, Midwest home whose good looks and quick wits carry him through the depression to Hollywood." —David Blundy and John Barnes of London's *Sunday Times Weekly Review*

The natural look was unusually genuine in Reagan's case. He wore no makeup in most of his films—it did not suit his complexion—nor did he wear it for television, either as an actor or a politician.

"In my first year and a half at Warner Brothers, I made thirteen pictures," Reagan would recall. "Usually, I was in and out of a movie in three or four weeks." The results were often forgettable, though lucrative for the studio. "I was proud of some of the B pictures we made," said Reagan, "but a lot of them were pretty poor. They were movies the studio didn't want good, they wanted 'em Thursday." Even so, the steady stream of B pictures gave the young actor considerable exposure, along with the chance to learn his craft and to work with some fine fellow actors. On the whole, Reagan respected the studio system, which had the resources to develop great stars over time. "This system turned out many of the best pictures ever made," he said. "Each studio was like a big family. You belonged to Warner Brothers or MGM or Paramount and your associates and friends were mostly other performers and writers and directors from your studio. Sometimes we had family fights, but the system gave a solid stability to the picture business. You belonged someplace."

Love Is on the Air, 1937

Accidents Will Happen, 1938

Hell's Kitchen, 1939

Smashing the Money Ring, 1939

The Bad Man, 1941

Million Dollar Baby, 1941

"Ronald Reagan is not only a brash reporter to end all screen reporters; he's also hilariously scatter-brained and devilishly resourceful. What he does to the opposition photographer shouldn't happen to a Giants fan in Brooklyn. Reagan gives a superbly helter-skelter performance." —*Variety,* review of *Nine Lives Are Not Enough,* September 1941

International Squadron, 1941

Stallion Road, 1947

That Hagen Girl, 1947

The Voice of the Turtle, 1947

The Girl from Jones Beach. 1949

Bedtime for Bonzo, 1951

The Winning Team, 1952

Law and Order, 1953

Cattle Queen of Montana, 1954

1937
Love Is on the Air

1938
Hollywood Hotel
Swing Your Lady
Sergeant Murphy
Accidents Will Happen
Cowboy from Brooklyn
Boy Meets Girl
Girls on Probation
Brother Rat

1939
Going Places
Secret Service of the Air
Dark Victory
Code of the Secret Service
Naughty but Nice
Hell's Kitchen
Angels Wash Their Faces
Smashing the Money Ring

1940
Brother Rat and a Baby
An Angel from Texas
Murder in the Air
Knute Rockne—All American
Tugboat Annie Sails Again
Santa Fe Trail

1941
The Bad Man
Million Dollar Baby
Nine Lives Are Not Enough
International Squadron

1942
Kings Row
Juke Girl
Desperate Journey

1943
This Is the Army

1947
Stallion Road
That Hagen Girl
The Voice of the Turtle

1949
John Loves Mary
Night Unto Night
The Girl from Jones Beach
It's a Great Feeling

1950
The Hasty Heart
Louisa

1951
Storm Warning
Bedtime for Bonzo
The Last Outpost

1952
Hong Kong
She's Working Her Way
   through College
The Winning Team

1953
Tropic Zone
Law and Order

1954
Prisoner of War
Cattle Queen of Montana

1955
Tennessee's Partner

1957
Hellcats of the Navy

1964
The Killers

During down time on the Warner Brothers set, Reagan enjoys a card game with some other young actors. Most of the time, however, Reagan spent his off-screen moments working, picking up acting tips from more experienced colleagues.

Reagan and Laraine Day were featured in the 1941 drama *The Bad Man*. The film's stars were accomplished veteran actors Wallace Beery and Lionel Barrymore.

"I feel very humble and not a little bit scared. Ever since I signed the contract and committed myself to at least a brief whirl at the movies, I've had the same sort of feeling that a man must have in death row. He knows he has to walk up the scaffold and take it in the neck and is anxious to get it over with quickly." —Ronald Reagan, in the *Des Moines Register*, 1937

At left, Reagan signs autographs on the set of *International Squadron*, a war movie released in 1941. Above, Reagan jokes off the set with costars Robert Horton, left, and Dewey Martin during the 1954 filming of *Prisoner of War*, based on the Korean War.

HIS VALUES "An actor knows two things—to be honest in what he's doing and to be in touch with the audience. That's not bad advice for a politician either."

—Ronald Reagan, in conversation with speechwriter Landon Parvin

Reagan appeared in the 1940 comedy *Tugboat Annie Sails Again,* the belated sequel to the popular 1933 film *Tugboat Annie.* Reagan, cast as "Eddie" the sailor, stands on deck with Marjorie Rambeau ("Annie") and Alan Hale ("Captain Bullwinkle").

LOVE IS ON THE AIR

CODE OF THE SECRET SERVICE

SUBMARINE D-1

SERGEANT MURPHY

SWING YOUR LADY

ACCIDENTS WILL HAPPEN

COWBOY FROM BROOKLYN

BOY MEETS GIRL

GIRLS ON PROBATION

GOING PLACES

DARK VICTORY

NAUGHTY BUT NICE

HELL'S KITCHEN

KNUTE ROCKNE

KING'S ROW

JUKE GIRL

DESPERATE JOURNEY

THIS IS THE ARMY

STALLION ROAD

THAT HAGEN GIRL

THE VOICE OF THE TURTLE

THE GIRL FROM JONES BEACH

JOHN LOVES MARY

NIGHT UNTO NIGHT

THE HASTY HEART

LOUISA

BEDTIME FOR BONZO

THE LAST OUTPOST

STORM WARNING

HONG KONG

SHE'S WORKING HER WAY THRU COLLEGE

THE WINNING TEAM

TROPIC ZONE

NINE LIVES ARE NOT ENOUGH

SANTA FE TRAIL

SECRET SERVICE IN THE AIR

SMASHING THE MONEY RING

HOLLYWOOD HOTEL

MILLION DOLLAR BABY

ANGELS WASH THEIR FACES

BROTHER RAT

BROTHER RAT AND THE BABY

ANGEL FROM TEXAS

INTERNATIONAL SQUADRON

"If some of it is largely sentimental and on the mock-heroic side; if some of it is slightly juvenile, that's all part of the sport. And that also makes it one of the best pictures for boys in years." —The *New York Times*, in a review of *Knute Rockne—All American,* 1940

Reagan's film debut was in 1937's *Love Is on the Air,* a frothy vehicle about a brash young radio newscaster demoted to a children's program. Based on the Broadway hit *Hi, Nellie,* the story was recycled several times by Hollywood. At left is Reagan's own Hollywood photo album, containing movie stills, such as this one from *Love Is on the Air,* and publicity shots. Lining the album jacket is a list of his movies, to date.

"*Love Is on the Air* presents a new leading man, Ronald Reagan, who is a natural, giving one of the best first picture performances Hollywood has offered in many a day."

—The *Hollywood Reporter,* 1937

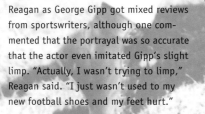

Reagan as George Gipp got mixed reviews from sportswriters, although one commented that the portrayal was so accurate that the actor even imitated Gipp's slight limp. "Actually, I wasn't trying to limp," Reagan said. "I just wasn't used to my new football shoes and my feet hurt."

"I've always suspected that there might have been actors in Hollywood who could have played the part better, but no one could have wanted to play it more than I did."

—Ronald Reagan, referring to the role of the Gipper

RONALD REAGAN—ALL AMERICAN

Just being a working actor may have once been his dream, but being a benchwarmer in B movies was not Ronald Reagan's style. So he set about creating his own breakout role.

He had long been intrigued with the story of Notre Dame's Knute Rockne, the Norwegian-born coach who, in the 1920s, revolutionized college football. Rockne had died in a plane crash while still fairly young, and his most famous player, George Gipp, had died even younger—expiring of pneumonia two weeks after his final game. The story had pathos and heroism aplenty. It could not miss. Reagan began writing a screenplay, with some definite casting ideas: For Rockne, Pat O'Brien, and for George Gipp, who else but Reagan himself?

He liked to talk up his idea around the Warners' commissary, so he should not have been surprised when he read in *Variety* that his studio had bought the rights to Rockne's life and was making a movie starring Pat O'Brien. Warners already had a wish list of ten actors for the part of George Gipp.

"I ran all the way to the producer's office and asked for a shot at the role," he would recall later. "He turned me down because he said I didn't look like the greatest football

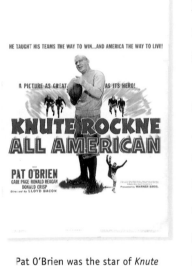

Pat O'Brien was the star of *Knute Rockne—All American*, but Reagan's death scene motivated the coach to deliver the famous "win one for the Gipper" speech.

player of our time. 'You mean Gipp has to weigh about two hundred pounds?' I asked. 'Would it surprise you that I'm five pounds heavier than George Gipp?'"

The producer was unconvinced, so Reagan rushed home, rummaged through his Eureka yearbooks, dashed back, and threw on the producer's desk a picture of himself in full football regalia. Two days later, he had the role.

Months thereafter, he sat in a Pasadena theater watching a sneak preview of *Knute Rockne—All American,* tension mounting during Gipp's dying speech: "Sometime, Rock, when the team's up against it, when things are wrong and the breaks are beating the boys, tell them to go in there with all they've got and win one for the Gipper. I don't know where I'll be then, Rock, but I'll know about it, and I'll be happy."

At the sounds of sniffles, Reagan relaxed. His relief was well founded. The studio called that night saying he was to star with Errol Flynn in the upcoming *Santa Fe Trail*—by any standard an A picture.

Weeks later, Reagan invited his father, Jack, now very ill, to attend the Rockne movie's premier at Notre Dame. It meant a lot to both father and son. Before dying soon thereafter, Jack proudly told Nelle, "I was there when our son became a star."

"At first, he had leading roles, but in B pictures, which filled the other half of the double features. Then came the kind of break every actor waits for. He was cast as George Gipp in the story of the great football coach Knute Rockne. Pat O'Brien starred in the title role. Ronnie only appeared in one reel; yet it was a perfect part. Knute Rockne *took him out of the B pictures once and for all."* —Nancy Reagan

"WHERE IS THE REST OF ME?"

Despite his fondness for *Knute Rockne—All American*, it was not Ronald Reagan's favorite. That distinction belonged to the complex and controversial melodrama *Kings Row*, released by Warners in 1942.

Based on a steamy novel by Henry Bellamann about a small turn-of-the-century American town, its darker aspects included murder, incest, nymphomania, insanity, sadism, larceny, euthanasia, suicide, and medical mutilation. It was toned down for the screen, but still considered racy for its time.

Reagan played wealthy, arrogant playboy Drake McHugh, who is loathed by the town's evil surgeon, Dr. Gordon (Charles Coburn). When Drake is hurt in a railroad accident, the doctor takes the purely sadistic opportunity to amputate his legs. Emerging from the anesthetic, Drake sees his limbs missing and screams to his lover (Ann Sheridan), "Randy, where is the rest of me?"

Reagan agonized over the scene for days. How could he communicate the terror? "At night I would wake up staring at the ceiling," he would recall, "and automatically mutter the line before I went back to sleep." At least on the fateful day of the scene he looked properly wan; the night before had been sleepless.

On the set he climbed onto a mattress. "When I got under the covers my legs went into the hollowed out section of the mattress," he said. "As I lay there looking down the length of the bed, it really looked like my body ended at the hips." He lay steady for the half-hour it took to light the scene, and his horror at the all-too-real illusion mounted. He muttered to director Sam Wood, "No rehearsal—just shoot it."

"Action," Wood called, and Reagan shrieked the line with conviction.

"Print it," said Wood.

His performance and the movie received critical acclaim. "Wonderful to this reviewer to see Ronald Reagan fulfill every promise," raved gossip queen Louella Parsons. "This is really Ronnie's big chance and he makes the most of it."

There was even talk of an Oscar. In those days, however, a studio usually threw its weight behind only one picture and one star, and that year Warners backed Jimmy Cagney in *Yankee Doodle Dandy*. Cagney won. No matter: For Reagan, his own picture was still an unqualified success.

A movie poster for *Kings Row* hints at the high melodrama of the film's passion-filled plot.

"*Kings Row* will give you that rare glow which comes from seeing a job well done crisply, competently, and with confidence. It has such distinction that it is plainly too good for the shoddy fellowship of the 'ten best pictures of the year.'" —*The New Yorker*, February 1941

"I still believe *Kings Row* is the finest picture I ever appeared in and it elevated me to the degree of stardom I had dreamed of when I had arrived in Hollywood four years earlier." —Ronald Reagan

The moment of tragedy in *Kings Row* comes as Drake (Reagan), reviving after surgery, discovers his legs gone. He shrieks to Randy (Ann Sheridan) the now-famous line, "Where is the rest of me?"

Reagan made *Hong Kong* with Rhonda Fleming for Paramount in 1952. He said their young costar, Danny Chang, was so fetching he felt upstaged.

In 1957's *Hellcats of the Navy,* Reagan, a submarine commander, appeared with Arthur Franz and with his costar for life, Nancy Davis.

ON THE SET

HIS VOICE "I was sitting around on the set with all these people and we were listening to Ronnie, quite absorbed. It wasn't a lecture—but he just got to talking and took the center of the stage. He's able to do that. And in the middle of his talk, there was a short pause and—I'll

Always accessible to his fans, above, Reagan was happy to sign autographs. Below, on the set of MGM's *Prisoner of War* in 1954, he is particularly attentive to a special fan, Nancy Davis Reagan. They had been married two years earlier.

never forget this— ... I said, 'Ron, have you ever considered someday becoming president?' And he said, 'President of what?' 'President of the United States,' I said. And he said, 'What's the matter—don't you like my acting, either?'" —Robert Cummings, actor

Sports fan Reagan loved making *The Winning Team* in 1952 with his friend Doris Day. He played baseball's legendary pitcher Grover Cleveland Alexander. Day played Alexander's wife, Aimee. At left is an original standee from the movie. Standees such as this were displayed in theater lobbies, some standing as tall as ten feet.

IN THE MOVIES

HIS VOICE "There were two things about Ronnie that impressed me—how much he liked to dance and how much he liked to talk. . . . I remember telling him that he should be touring the country making speeches. He was very good at it." —Doris Day, actor

Tender scenes between Reagan and Day, left, depicted the Alexanders' troubled love story, which was central to *The Winning Team*. Above, Reagan tells a story to entertain fellow actors Alan Hale (left), Arthur Kennedy (right), and a bit player during the filming of Warner Brothers' *Desperate Journey*, a World War II picture.

"Ronnie was like a rock. He had depth and character; he was low-key.... And he could keep things moving. He'd keep people occupied with his storytelling. There was no boring time on the set with Ronnie. He kept the energy level up." —Rhonda Fleming, actor

SAG president Ronald Reagan speaks at a union gathering in 1948. His listeners include, left to right, disavowed communist Howard Costigan; Roy Brewer, chair of the Hollywood AFL Film Council; and actress (and later congresswoman) Helen Gahagan Douglas.

HIS VISION "American movies occupied 70 percent of all the playing time on the world's movie screens in those first years after World War II, and, as was to become more and more apparent to me, Joseph Stalin had set out to make Hollywood an instrument of propaganda for his program of Soviet

STATE OF THE UNION

At the outset, the man who would come to lead his labor union to some great victories did not even want to be a member. "When I arrived in Hollywood, actors and actresses had just won a tough five-year battle with studios for the union shop and recognition of the Screen Actors Guild as the exclusive bargaining agent for actors," Ronald Reagan said. "Like all contract players, I'd had to join the union and wasn't very happy about it. Making me join the union, whether I wanted to or not, I thought, was an infringement on my rights."

Yet talking with older colleagues he soon learned how, during the pre-SAG days, the studios had grossly exploited lesser-known actors—and he began to change his mind. He became convinced when drafted to serve on SAG's board of directors, representing young contract players. Attending his first board meeting, he expected to find a group of unknowns. Instead, there were Cary Grant, Jimmy Cagney, and several other top stars, "who didn't need the Guild's help to negotiate their wages," Reagan said. "But they enthusiastically gave their time and prestige to assure that lesser players like me got a fair shake. That night I told myself that if I ever became a star, I'd do as much as I could to help the actors and actresses at the bottom of the ladder."

After he returned from military service, Reagan resumed his place on the SAG board. About the same time, he began speaking out about domestic fascism. He had been horrified by Nazism abroad, and he wanted to help prevent its taking root at home. To that end, he also joined several organizations in Hollywood that shared his views, inveighing against fascism to enthusiastic applause. But later, when he denounced communism as well, the reaction ranged from tepid to hostile.

This disturbed him, as did the growing evidence he found that communists were trying to infiltrate Hollywood labor unions, and through them the movie industry itself. Still a liberal Democrat in those days, he had generally viewed American communists as relatively harmless malcontents, for the most part well intentioned but misguided. Now he was changing his mind.

"For a long time, I believed the best way to beat the communists was through the forces of liberal democracy," he said, "which had just defeated Hitler's brand of totalitarianism. . . . But I was to discover that a lot of 'liberals'

Ronald and Nancy Reagan listen to SAG founding member Kenneth Thomson's speech at a 1960 strike settlement meeting.

expansionism aimed at communizing the world. . . . More than anything else, it was the communists' attempted takeover of Hollywood and its worldwide weekly audience of more than five hundred million people that led me to accept a nomination to serve as president of the Screen Actors Guild and, indirectly at least, set me on the road that would lead me into politics." —Ronald Reagan

just couldn't accept the notion that Moscow had bad intentions or wanted to take over Hollywood and many other American industries through subversion, or that Stalin was a murderous gangster. To them, fighting totalitarianism was 'witch hunting' and 'red baiting.'"

In that vein, Reagan himself was much criticized for his crusade against communist influence in Hollywood—particularly for cooperating with the House Un-American Activities Committee (HUAC), the force behind the infamous Hollywood blacklisting of suspected communists or communist sympathizers. But he knew that there were two blacklists, the second kept by the communists and aimed at destroying their enemies' careers. They had threatened to end his, in fact, by throwing acid in his face.

And while he did cooperate with HUAC's investigation, Reagan never "named names"—implicated any individual as being a communist—and he was aware of HUAC's excesses, acknowledging that some members "came to Hollywood searching more for personal publicity than they were for communists." He continued, "Many fine people were accused wrongly of being communists simply because they were liberals." Reagan spearheaded SAG's effort to help clear the falsely accused. Moreover, when he testified before HUAC in 1947, he warned against throwing out the First Amendment in the name of anticommunism. "As a citizen," he said, "I would hesitate, or not like, to see any political party outlawed on the basis of its political ideology. We have spent 170 years in this country on the basis that democracy is strong enough to stand up and fight against the inroads of any ideology."

Reagan had become much more conservative than most of Hollywood. Nevertheless, his colleagues respected him and elected him president of SAG in 1947. He was reelected to four successive terms, then called back in 1959 to lead the union's first strike against the studios. It was an unqualified success: The union won pension and medical plans, as well as much-deserved and highly lucrative residual payments for actors in films that the studios subsequently sold to television.

However they viewed his politics in later years, most SAG members agreed—Ronald Reagan was one of the best presidents the union ever had.

At a January 1952 SAG board meeting, Guild president Reagan addresses the board and staff, including Nancy Davis. She would become his wife two months later.

HIS VALUES "He was not just a lucky and blessed young man, a bright fellow smiled on by the gods. He had grit. . . . Just when everyone else was going left, particularly everyone in Hollywood who could enhance his career, he was going right. But he held to his position."

—Peggy Noonan, author and Reagan speechwriter

"I respected him for the role that he took in the Screen Actors Guild in working for the actors and their cause during those uneasy times. I think that he did a very good job for the actors guild. He was working for the actors—he wasn't doing it for political reasons, because he wasn't interested in national politics yet." —Jimmy Stewart, actor

Reagan chats with Gene Kelly and Anna Roosevelt at a 1947 meeting of the League of Hollywood Voters. Dancer-actor Kelly was vice president of SAG when Reagan was first president. Roosevelt was the daughter of Reagan's boyhood idol, FDR.

Nancy Reagan admires an award presented to her husband by the Screen Actors Guild during SAG's annual membership meeting on November 21, 1960. Reagan had resigned as Guild president in June after leading the union through the most successful strike in its history.

"Let me say here that I believe in the SAG with all my heart. It is a damned noble organization: I mean exactly that. It demonstrates in practical terms the instinctive brotherhood which exists in show business." —Ronald Reagan

The Reagans embrace, at left, as they leave the Beverly Hilton Hotel, where Reagan received the SAG award. As his award acknowledged, Reagan had, as he said, successfully "matched wits with some of the shrewdest negotiators on the planet"—and won.

Reagan confers with his rank and file, above, at a SAG strike meeting at the Hollywood Palladium. One veteran of the strike days once commented that the gains Reagan won for the union helped pay for most of the houses in the San Fernando Valley.

"I found Ronald Reagan to be a very skilled negotiator, not least because he was always good-humored. He would never take a confrontational position; he was not dogmatic. He might disagree, but he'd find a way to leave the other side with a feeling that they were good guys, too, and not the enemy." —Charlton Heston, actor and former SAG board member

The luminous appeal of young actress Nancy Davis is captured in a publicity photo. She gave up her film career when she married Ronald Reagan. Her greatest ambition, she always said, was to have a good marriage.

"It was because of the Guild and, more precisely, because I was president, that I found myself standing before an apartment door in Westwood one pleasant fall evening. When that door opened, I found all the rest of me I needed to find to give me more happiness than any one person could possibly deserve." —Ronald Reagan

NANCY

As the 1950s began, Ronald Reagan's public life as actor and SAG president was busy and rewarding, but his personal life was in limbo. A bachelor again, he lived alone in a pleasant Hollywood apartment and spent many pleasant evenings in nearby nightclubs, dining with various young women, all of them pleasant—and yet interchangeable and unimportant. If there was some vacancy in his life, he was too busy to notice. It was pleasant enough; he had no plans to change.

Then a call came one day from director Mervyn LeRoy, who wanted a favor. A young MGM contract player named Nancy Davis had seen her name on the membership lists of several communist front groups and was very upset about the apparent mix-up in names. Would Reagan, as SAG president, look into it? He did, found that the name indeed belonged to another Nancy Davis, and called LeRoy back with the assurance that Miss Davis was in the clear.

"She's still worried that people are going to think she's a communist," pressed LeRoy. "Why don't you give her a call? I think she will take it better from you than from me."

Reagan agreed to phone her and explain things over dinner, but he was not taking any chances.

The Reagans' wedding certificate is now displayed in the Ronald Reagan Presidential Library.

"I have an early call in the morning," he fibbed to Nancy, "so I'm afraid we'll have to make it an early evening."

"Fine," she fibbed back. "I've got an early call, too. I can't stay out too late either."

Half expecting to be greeted by a stereotypical starlet, Reagan was both surprised and pleased at what he saw. She was a tiny, delicate, lovely young woman with dark hair and wide-spaced hazel eyes. The "early evening" stretched on toward 3:00 A.M. as they talked and got acquainted.

Like him, she was from the Midwest, but their childhoods had been very different. She was born Anne Frances Robbins but preferred her childhood nickname, "Nancy." Her mother, Edith Luckett, was an actress who often traveled, performing on stage and in radio. Her parents divorced soon after Nancy's birth, and the man Nancy revered as her father was Edith's second husband, the eminent Chicago neurosurgeon Loyal Davis, who had adopted her. After graduating from Smith College, Nancy had come to Hollywood in the 1940s and had appeared in several films for MGM.

Of her dinner companion that evening, Nancy was intrigued to find that he was "less like an actor than anyone

"Mervyn assured me that Ronnie was a nice young man and I was a nice young woman, and it might be nice if we met. Well, I had seen him in films and, frankly, I had liked what I had seen; so I, too, said I thought that would be very nice. I wanted to meet Ronald Reagan." —Nancy Reagan

I had known." Possibly expecting egotism and tunnel-vision shoptalk from this established star, she found something much different. "One of the things I liked about Ronnie right away was that he didn't talk only about himself," she would recall. "He told me about the Guild, and why the actors' union meant so much to him. He talked about his small ranch in the San Fernando Valley, about horses and their bloodlines; he was also a Civil War buff, and he knew a lot about wine.

"I don't know if it was love at first sight," she later assessed, "but it was something close to it."

Reagan was enchanted with her, too, but—ever the loner at heart—he was also wary. After that first night they continued to date, but not exclusively. It took a little time for him to realize that the only woman he really wanted to see was Nancy. When he did, his proposal was simple.

"Let's get married," he said one night over dinner. She put her hand in his. "Let's."

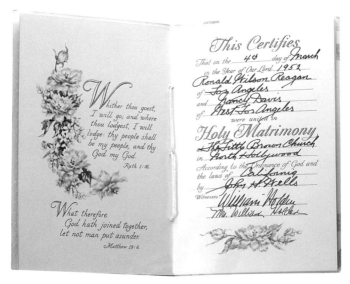

The inside of their wedding certificate bears the signatures of the principals at the Reagans' modest wedding, including those of the bride, groom, and their two attendants, actor William Holden and his wife, Ardis.

On March 4, 1952, they were wed in a small, quiet ceremony in the Little Brown Church in the San Fernando Valley.

It may have taken time for Ronald Reagan to realize he was in love, but thereafter his devotion was deep, complete, and forever. Known for his rhetorical powers, he was never more eloquent than when he spoke or wrote about his wife.

"If ever God gave me evidence that He had a plan for me, it was the night He brought Nancy into my life," he would say. "It is almost impossible for me to express fully how deeply I love Nancy and how much she has filled my life. Nancy moved into my heart and replaced an emptiness that I'd been trying to ignore for a long time. Coming home to her is like coming out of the cold into a warm, firelit room."

Echoing his wife's sentiment, he would also attest, "Sometimes I think my life really began when I met Nancy."

HIS VALUES *"He has always been sentimental. He used to send flowers to Mother on my birthday—to thank her for giving birth to me. On Valentine's Day, my birthday, or our anniversary, I'll find half a dozen cards from Ronnie waiting for me at breakfast. Often he writes at the bottom,*

'I.T.W.W.W.,' which stands for 'in the whole wide world.' As in: 'I love you more than anything I.T.W.W.W.'" —Nancy Reagan

The newlyweds cut the cake at the Holdens' after the ceremony. Ardis Holden arranged for the cake and photographer. "Thank heaven for Ardis," Reagan said, "because my plans hadn't gotten beyond 'I do.'"

A wedding day kiss is caught on this photograph from Nancy Reagan's private collection. The couple honeymooned in Phoenix, at Nancy's request; her family had a tradition of spending spring vacations there.

"It's the most real love I've ever seen. What you see there is right. It is true. Reagan said once that his life began when he met Nancy, and I believe that to be true. I think that he became a fulfilled person. He became able to do many things that he wanted to do because of Nancy." —Michael Deaver, deputy chief of staff

The new Mrs. Reagan smiles happily for the camera in this photo from Nancy Reagan's private collection.

The Reagans relax at their home in Pacific Palisades, purchased shortly after their marriage. "At the time," Nancy would recall, "nobody could understand why we were moving way out there—'in the country,' as it was thought of then."

If Nancy Davis hadn't come along when she did, I would have lost my soul." —Ronald Reagan

Vacationing in Coronado, near San Diego, the Reagans enjoy the sun and sand. As governor and first lady of California a few years later, right, they would have less time for such getaways.

"My parents have about as close a relationship as I've ever seen anyone have. They really, sort of complete each other. They're kind of two halves of a circle." —Patti Davis, daughter

"We go back a long way with Ronald Reagan. To before he was ever thinking of running for public office, when he was working for General Electric. And they were such a great couple, Ronnie and Nancy. They've always been exactly the same." —Marion Jorgensen, family friend

"The Reagans and
Mary Jane and I
have been good
friends for a
long time and
have shared a lot
of happy times
together. As
I look over
Ronald Reagan's
years in the
public limelight,
I think the secret
of his success is
his enormous
personal integrity,
together with the
incomparable
support of his
beloved Nancy."

—Charles Z. Wick, director of
the United States Information
Agency

Though still newly married in 1957, the Reagans were about to have a full house. Nancy gave birth to their second child, Ron, shortly after this picture was taken, and the same year Ron was born, Reagan's teenage son Michael would come to live with the growing family, which included daughter Patti, then about five years old. Only Maureen, Reagan's oldest, was away from home at the time, attending a Catholic high school on the East Coast.

The Reagans enjoy a spectacular view from the deck of their second Pacific Palisades house, at left, where they moved in 1957. The property afforded vistas of the Pacific Ocean, the mountains, and the city of Los Angeles. It also had a pool (above) that Ronald Reagan enjoyed. The family owned the house until 1981, holding on to it even during Reagan's two terms as governor in Sacramento.

HIS VALUES *"Ronnie needed a lot of moral support when we first were married. Kings Row made him a star while he was in the service, but for more than four years he was unable to follow up on it. Returning from the Army Air Force, he found*

CROSSROADS

After World War II, Ronald Reagan had returned to a Hollywood that would never be quite the same. The era in which the seven major studios had the money to find, train, and publicize great and enduring stars—the Clark Gables and Jimmy Stewarts and Bette Davises and Joan Crawfords—was over.

One reason was a Justice Department antitrust edict decreeing that the studios could either make movies or operate theaters, but not both. Deprived at once of revenue and a reliable outlet for their films, the studios were much less willing or able to take risks on pictures or personnel. Adding to the problem was television, so recently a novelty but fast becoming a staple. Many moviegoers now preferred to stay home and be entertained for free.

Under these conditions, many actors, including Reagan, let their studio contracts lapse and went freelance. To most, it made sense financially, giving them more control over when and how much they worked. Stars like Reagan were in the 91 percent tax bracket, and they found the government biting deep into their incentive to work more and earn more.

At the same time, Reagan was finding fewer offers to his liking. He made twenty-two of his fifty-three films after the war, but the momentum from his high point in *Kings Row* had dwindled during his years away. And he believed his union activism was costing him roles in a subtle form of stereotyping.

"They stop thinking of you as an actor," he said. "The image they have of you isn't associated with your last role, but with the guy who sat across the conference table, beefing. And that's death! You develop a sort of aura. People even forget in time how you came to have it. Your name just doesn't come up when parts are being discussed."

There was television, but Reagan, like most movie stars, was leery of it. The overexposure it entailed could kill a film career, especially if the audience came to associate the actor with a particular role. But in 1954, he received the perfect TV offer: The General Electric Company was planning to produce a weekly dramatic anthology, the *GE Theater*. The company wanted him to host the show every week and star in an occasional program.

It was a lucrative opportunity, and it avoided the type-casting problem. In retrospect, though, these inducements would pale beside another factor: *GE Theater* would provide both a platform and a training ground for one of Reagan's lifelong and increasing interests—politics.

Boating off Coronado in 1962, Reagan holds son Ron in his lap.

himself all but forgotten. He began to freelance and was offered a lot of films but few good ones. We talked it over and decided to wait for better opportunities. We were worried about the direction his career and Hollywood in general were going. Waiting it out without working was hard on the budget, but we got by." —Nancy Reagan

HIS VISION "As far back as I can remember, Ronnie was always interested in the issues of the day.... He wasn't just a Hollywood star. He was a thinking man. And a lot of people, I think, didn't realize that." —Lee Annenberg, White House chief of protocol and family friend

Still looking like newlyweds, the Reagans stroll along a pier at Lake Mead, Nevada, in 1954. A week earlier, Reagan had celebrated his forty-third birthday. He was about to embark on his television career.

A Voice for California

"We cannot, must not,

About the time he switched from movies to television, Ronald Reagan was reaching the end stage of a change far more significant, one that would allow him a new avenue to express his views— a change in his political affiliations that would redirect the course of his life.

He had inherited his political views from his father, an ardent populist and New Deal Democrat whose chief concern was that the American worker get a fair shake. Like Jack, the young Ronald Reagan distrusted big business and relied on government to solve the nation's problems.

"Probably because of my dad's influence and my experiences during the depression, I had loved the Democratic Party," Reagan would say. "I agreed with Thomas Jefferson, its founder, who said: 'Democrats consider the people as the safest depository of power in the last resort; they cherish them, therefore, and wish to leave in them all the powers to the exercise of which they are competent.'"

Reagan had come to believe, though, that the Democratic Party was abandoning both Jefferson and him. The early Democrats had espoused individual liberties and small government. But during the 1930s, Reagan believed the party had begun "creating a government that grew ever larger and increasingly demanded the right to regulate and plan the social and economic life of the country and move into arenas best left to private enterprise."

and will not turn back."

"I guess I was beginning to form one of my own principles about government," he said. "There probably isn't any undertaking on earth short of assuring the national security that can't be handled more efficiently by the forces of private enterprise than by the federal government." He had witnessed the foibles of big-government bureaucracy, first in the excesses of the New Deal and then in the army. After the war, filming *The Hasty Heart* in England under the Labour Party, he "saw firsthand how the welfare state sapped incentive to work from many people in a wonderful and dynamic country."

These experiences, along with what he regarded as the naïveté of his leftist Hollywood friends in denying the threat of communism, had left him disenchanted with liberalism and fearful that America was drifting toward a socialism that could extinguish individual liberty. A government big enough to take care of you, he believed, was also big enough to swallow your life.

That was his frame of mind in 1954 when he began his eight-year stint hosting *GE Theater*. At this crossroad, too, fate seemed to be steering his course, for his new job involved duties beyond the entertainment industry. It entailed visiting GE's many plants throughout the country—"as a kind of goodwill ambassador from the home office," he said. At first he chatted with the workers mostly about Hollywood, but politics and social issues gradually edged out all other subject matter. And he didn't just talk to the people: He listened to them, learning that many shared his views and concerns.

By 1964 his conversion from Democrat to Republican was complete—as was his evolution from veteran actor to apprentice politician—and he actively backed Republican senator Barry Goldwater's run for the presidency. Goldwater would lose in an avalanche victory to incumbent Democrat Lyndon Johnson. But the eloquence of Reagan's speeches so impressed California's most powerful Republicans that they urged him to run for governor.

Reagan was reluctant. "At fifty-four," he said, "the last thing I wanted to do was start a new career." Ultimately, however, he could not ignore the groundswell of support for him. He ran, and despite his opponents' sneers that he was a lightweight, a mere actor whose reach was vastly exceeding his grasp, he unseated the popular incumbent.

Sailing to the top of his state's hierarchy, Reagan entered politics' roiling waters at their most turbulent: in the mid-1960s, the most anguished and polarized time since the Civil War. Standing fast against student unrest on California's campuses and trying to curtail the state's ever-expanding government, he would find himself loved—and hated—on a massive scale.

He found it invigorating. He loved the job.

HIS VALUES "I had been a lifelong Democrat until the 1960s.... But one day I came home from a speaking trip and said to Nancy that it had just dawned on me that I had been making these speeches on what I thought was wrong with government and then every four years I'd

campaign for people who were doing these things. So I finally changed parties, and in 1964 I became cochairman for Californians for Barry Goldwater, the Republican presidential candidate." —Ronald Reagan

The Reagans, both devoted to the outdoor life, enjoy a boating excursion in the mid-1960s. His acting career was all but over by this time, and he was about to enter a new arena.

Reagan talks with GE workers. Though he traveled extensively, he had it written into his contract that he not be asked to fly. He feared plane crashes, and only began to fly after becoming governor years later.

"In the fifties and early sixties, while the other people in power in the eighties were joining government and learning its language, he was going from plant to plant for GE, shooting the breeze with the workers

THE POLITICAL APPRENTICE

Ronald Reagan's roving ambassadorship for his new employer started modestly enough. He would visit a plant and walk the assembly line, talking with workers in small groups, telling them about *GE Theater* and regaling them with some Hollywood yarns. But a year or two into the tours, things began to change. Visiting a plant whose workers had been raising funds for charity, he gave a speech about the virtues of individual giving as opposed to government aid. The applause was so enthusiastic that GE decided to expand his audience.

"From then on," Reagan would relate, "whenever I went to a GE plant, in addition to meeting workers, they'd schedule a speech or two for me to a local organization like the United Fund or Chamber of Commerce; before long, the company began to get requests for me to speak before larger audiences—state conventions of service organizations and groups like the Executives Club in Chicago and the Commonwealth Club in San Francisco."

As the audiences changed, so did the speech. He began recounting how governmental tampering had hurt the movie industry and warning that what had happened in Hollywood could happen elsewhere. The response was

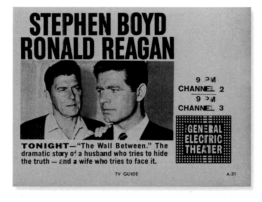

A *TV Guide* ad promotes one of the *GE Theater* episodes for which Reagan was star as well as host.

electric. "No matter where I was," he would say, "I'd find people from the audience waiting to talk to me after a speech and they'd all say, 'Hey, if you think things are bad in your business, let me tell you what is happening in my business. . . .'" In this symbiotic give and take, his own views began taking on their final form as he saw firsthand the government's role in the lives of the American people. The movies steadily shrank from his speeches until finally, he said, "the Hollywood part just got lost and I was out there beating the bushes for private enterprise."

GE Theater ended its run in 1962, and in 1964 Reagan made his last film, *The Killers*. Then he took on another television series, hosting and sometimes starring in *Death Valley Days*.

But his acting career was coming to an end, and he was on the threshold of another pivotal, life-changing event. Reagan's philosophy of individual freedom and responsibility closely tracked Senator Barry Goldwater's thinking, and in 1964 Reagan agreed to cochair the Arizona Republican's presidential campaign in California. The job involved fund-raising and making speeches—one of which would start Reagan down his own road to the White House.

---

in the cafeteria, the guys on the line telling him what they thought. More than any president since Jackson, he spent the years before power with the people, the normal people of his country."

—Peggy Noonan, author and Reagan speechwriter

Reagan looks dapper in this *GE Theater* publicity photo. His major movie star presence on the small screen helped make the program a Sunday night staple in many American living rooms during its long eight-year run.

"For eight years I hopscotched around the country by train and automobile for GE and visited every one of its 139 plants, some of them several times. Along the way, I met more than 250,000 employees of GE.... Looking back now, I realize it wasn't a bad apprenticeship for someone who'd someday enter public life." —Ronald Reagan

Model 202WGN. 19-inch (overall diagonal), 175 square inches of viewable picture.

Ronald Reagan introduces the CELEBRITY: "This General Electric portable television packs console performance into a 19-inch set at a sweet, low price. Why, the Celebrity works wherever a console will with its mighty new chassis and full-power transformer. And what a picture! Daylight Blue. The same crisp beauty you see on the noblest General Electric consoles." And built to live up to General Electric's record of trustworthiness: a study of television sets over a three-year period proved that General Electric sets needed less service than any other leading brand. All this for only $159.95. More, too—for a limited time only, most General Electric dealers are offering a smart plaid carry-cover with the Celebrity portable. See this star perform . . . today.

$159.95
UHF extra.

Manufacturer's suggested retail price $159.95. Slightly higher South, West, Hawaii and Alaska.

NEW 19-INCH PORTABLE

Progress Is Our Most Important Product

GENERAL ⓖⓔ ELECTRIC

TELEVISION RECEIVER DEPT.   SYRACUSE, NEW YORK   Custom-made carry-cover

"If you believe, as Ronnie does, that everything happens for a purpose, then there was certainly a hidden purpose in Ronnie's job with General Electric."

—Nancy Reagan

Vital to the company image, Reagan also appeared in GE's print advertising. When the Reagans built their second home in Pacific Palisades, GE insisted on making it an all-electric showcase. "They provided us with so many refrigerators, ovens, and fancy lights," said Nancy Reagan, "not to mention a built-in garbage disposal, that they had to build a special panel on the side of the house for all the wiring and the switches."

GENERAL ELECTRIC THEATER

HIS VOICE "GE was perfect for him. And the reason it was is that he was able to get out on the road and talk to people at a long distance from anybody else—speeches that were rarely covered, and if covered at all, were covered in the town newspaper. No national coverage. And he was free to make mistakes. It was a kind of apprenticeship that isn't there for most people, and he made the most of it." —Lou Cannon, journalist and Reagan biographer

Goldwater addresses a 1963 Young Republicans rally in San Francisco. His overwhelming defeat in the presidential race was a catastrophe for Republicans, but it helped launch Reagan's political career.

HIS VOICE "Probably what impressed the American people was that they'd been listening to these two politicians out there, Barry Goldwater and Lyndon Johnson, and all of a sudden, here's a man who

A TIME FOR CHOOSING

In 1964, Ronald Reagan addressed some eight hundred Republicans at a fund-raising dinner in Los Angeles. It was essentially the same speech he had honed over the years for GE: that America was at a crossroads, poised uneasily between freedom and socialism; that government was encroaching on what freedom was left; and that the threat from the Soviet Union was real and the Cold War must be won. The speech was so successful that, afterward, a group of Republican contributors asked if Reagan would repeat it for national television if they could raise the money for the airtime. He agreed, and on October 27, the speech was filmed in an NBC studio before a Republican audience. It would not elect Barry Goldwater president, but Reagan's eloquent and passionate words would launch his own political career, not as an opinion maker but as a candidate. Here is an excerpt from that speech:

"We are at war with the most dangerous enemy that has ever faced mankind in his long climb from the swamp to the stars, and it has been said that if we lose that war, and in doing so lose this way of freedom of ours, history will record with the greatest astonishment that those of us who had the most to lose did the least to prevent its happening. . . .

"This is the issue of this election: Whether we believe in our capacity for self-government or whether we abandon the American revolution and confess that a little intellectual elite in a far-distant capital can plan our lives for us better than we can plan them ourselves. . . . Those who would trade our freedom for the soup kitchen of the welfare state have told us that they have a utopian solution of peace without victory. They call their policy 'accommodation.' And they say if we can only avoid any direct confrontation with the enemy, he will forget his evil ways and learn to love us. . . .

"We cannot buy our security, our freedom from the threat of the bomb by committing an immorality so great as saying to a billion people now in slavery behind the Iron Curtain, 'Give up your dreams of freedom because to save our own skin, we are willing to make a deal with your slave masters.' . . . You and I have a rendezvous with destiny. We will preserve for our children this, the last best hope of man on earth, or we will sentence them to take the last step into a thousand years of darkness."

INDIVIDUAL LIBERTY

★

At the core of Reagan's famous speech was individual liberty. As he saw it, the government had limited the rights of Americans for too long. It was time to curb its growth. Once in office, he did just that, lowering taxes and downsizing federal programs. In his 1989 farewell address, the president reaffirmed: "Man is not free unless government is limited. There's a clear cause and effect here that is as neat and predictable as a law of physics: As government expands, liberty contracts." And he would do all he could to safeguard that freedom.

is saying some things that they believed, or a lot of them believed, [and he] was saying them in a very reasonable manner. He wasn't shouting, he wasn't demanding or anything, and of course, he was well known: Ronald Reagan, the actor and the movie star." —Lyn Nofziger, political and communications adviser

REAGAN FOR GOVERNOR

In the spring of 1965, the same group of Republicans who had financed the airing of Ronald Reagan's speech for Barry Goldwater visited Reagan and urged him to run for governor against the two-term Democratic incumbent, Pat Brown. Reagan was, they said, the only man who could unite California's Republican Party, fractured along moderate-conservative lines since Goldwater's disastrous loss the year before. Reagan was not exactly receptive.

"I almost laughed them out of the house," he would recall. "I said, in effect: 'You're out of your mind.'" Happy with their personal status quo, the Reagans were not looking for change. "We had our children, our friends in Hollywood, our home, our ranch, our privacy," Reagan said. "We had a good income and all the opportunities I ever wanted to speak about the issues that concerned me."

But the pressure was unrelenting, and he finally made a deal with his would-be backers: He would travel the state making speeches for six months and see what the people had to say before making a final decision. As it turned out, the people had the same advice everywhere: Run. In the end, he could not refuse. He won the Republican primary and

Reagan the gubernatorial candidate is featured in the June 9, 1966, edition of the *Saturday Evening Post*.

moved on to face Pat Brown in the general election.

Brown was happy to oppose Reagan. The liberal Democrat had won his first term against Richard Nixon and his second against Senator William F. Knowland. After that, he reasoned, this political novice—this actor—should be easy pickings. But he found to his dismay that Reagan had a knack for turning apparent liabilities into assets.

To Brown's charge of inexperience, Reagan happily agreed. "Sure," he said. "The man who has the job has more experience than anyone else . . . that's why I'm running." This strategy—presenting himself as an outsider eager to unsnarl the mess made by the professional politicians—turned out to be highly effective.

So did his method of facing Brown's assault that he was "only an actor who memorizes speeches written by other people." In fact, Reagan was writing his own speeches. Nevertheless, he began jettisoning his formal talks in favor of question-and-answer sessions with his audiences. The approach "worked like a charm," he said, proving that his views were neither scripted nor shallow.

On election day, the outcome was not even close: Reagan garnered 58 percent of the vote, Brown 42.

HIS VISION "I am an ordinary citizen with a deep-seated belief that much of what troubles us has been brought about by politicians; and it's high time that more ordinary citizens brought the fresh air of common-sense thinking to bear on these problems."

—Ronald Reagan, on the pre-campaign trail for governor.

"So what's this empty nonsense I hear about Ronald Reagan being 'just an actor'? I watched Ronald work most of his adult life preparing for public service. His will be a new, informed, vigorously dedicated leadership. So on November 8th, vote for Ronald Reagan." —John Wayne, in a TV endorsement for Reagan's first campaign for governor

Ron and Nancy take time to greet some voters-to-be during the first gubernatorial campaign. Once Reagan decided to enter the race, he found he actually liked campaigning. "And I was out to win," he said.

Reagan and incumbent governor Pat Brown, at top, briefly interrupt their hard-fought campaign to share an amiable moment during a 1966 interview. Below, Reagan speaks to supporters on familiar turf—Hollywood.

REGAIN RESPONSIBLE GOVERN[MENT] REAGA[N]

REAGAN CITIZENS' TRUST FUND 1011

CAPITOL OUTDOOR

For Governor...
Ronald
REAGAN

CALIFORNIA'S NEXT GOVERNOR

He would finish [his] speech and people would come up and ask for his autograph and I would say, you know, Ron, we've got to get out of here. We've got to go. 'Well, just a minute,' and he would sign every darn autograph that people asked for. He was just an instinctually nice man who attracted people to him and he was articulate and he was a man of conviction. No, there was never anything phony about Ronald Reagan." Lyn Nofziger, political and communications advisor

Our Next Govenor

"I felt sure the people would accept me as a campaigner for someone else, but not as a candidate myself. . . . The people had a different idea."

—Ronald Reagan

Reagan's first run for governor had all the usual campaign paraphernalia and practices—billboards and buttons, signs and stickers, speeches and interviews. But there was at least one departure from the norm: This candidate wrote his own speeches, and they said, without compromise, exactly what he thought and believed.

"In retrospect, I believe it benefited the country when I lost the governorship to him because, had I won, he would not have become president."

—George Christopher, former mayor of San Francisco and 1966 political opponent

At his 1967 inauguration, Governor Reagan was frank about California's woeful economy. "We are going to squeeze and cut and trim until we reduce the cost of government," he promised grimly.

"After years of criticizing government, I was about to stick my head into the lions' den and the lions would be waiting for me."

—Ronald Reagan

FACING THE LIONS

Optimist though he was, Ronald Reagan had not really expected to win the governorship. Now at the helm of a state bigger than many countries, he had to learn fast, and he quickly sought out the best help he could find. He called on some of California's top businesspeople to form a committee that would scrutinize state government, targeting problems and solutions. The committee went right to work—and turned up a glut of bad news.

To begin with, California was broke. The previous administration had concealed the fact that, for some time, the state had been hemorrhaging a million dollars a day more than it took in. Now it faced a debt of at least two hundred million dollars, and within two weeks of his January 2, 1967, inauguration, Reagan was supposed to submit a balanced budget to the legislature.

He immediately instituted a hiring freeze, a 10 percent across-the-board budget cut for state bureaucracies, and several other belt-tightening measures that won him enemies among Democratic lawmakers who controlled both the Assembly and the Senate. But when even these stringent moves could not cure what he called California's "worst financial crisis since the depression," Reagan was

The Reagan family welcomes Michigan governor George Romney and his wife during a 1967 press conference at the Reagans' home.

forced to resort to what he most abhorred: raising taxes.

In the end he would reverse the fiscal tide, curing the state's deficit and eventually even creating a surplus—money that, over the legislature's howls of protest, he returned in four separate rebates to California's taxpayers. It was, he pointed out, their money in the first place.

Yet money was not the only troublesome issue he faced. "We kept uncovering problems nobody had told me about," he said. "There was continuing violence on our campuses; Democratic legislators rejected my proposals right and left; moderates and conservatives in my own party couldn't get along; and I made lots of mistakes because of inexperience."

But he was learning, and he methodically attacked the problems with common sense and a management style he believed in: Delegate authority and don't interfere unless someone "drops the ball."

With his staff, he then turned to his goals of cutting spending, reducing the size of state government and making it more responsive to the people, bringing racial equity to state hiring, reforming welfare, and restoring calm to California's fractious college campuses at a time when dissent was sweeping across America like wildfire.

"People said to us in the beginning that there was not going to be such a change between the life we had led in pictures and politics. That was a lot of nonsense. There was a great deal of change. Your life is much more public. You have much less free time. In pictures, at least in the days when my husband was in them, you were more protected. And you're certainly not protected in politics." —Nancy Reagan

Reagan's first term gets off to a stylish start as California's new first couple heads for a 1967 inaugural gala.

Governor and Mrs. Reagan enjoy some private time in this late 1960s photo. The Reagans moved to the suburbs shortly after arriving in Sacramento, where, as Nancy Reagan said, their youngest son, Ron, "could have a normal life."

"Sometime after I'd become governor, and we were sitting in the living room, all of a sudden it came to both of us that what we were doing made everything else we'd ever done seem dull as dishwater." —Ronald Reagan

HIS VALUES "When he was governor, we were walking the streets of New York City when a man thrust a pencil and paper at him, politely asking for an autograph by saying, 'Please, Mr. Milland.' Reagan cheerfully signed the paper, 'Ray Milland.' As we walked away, I asked why he didn't tell the man who he really was. 'Why?' he said. 'I know who I am.'" —Michael Deaver, deputy chief of staff

"The room was lined with bookcases filled with books…. Most of the books were on economics, history, and politics. I said to myself, 'If this man is serious about what he stands for and is so charismatic that the crowds virtually glow when he is near them, then he is bound for big things nationally.' I thought, 'President,' and wrote it in my notebook."

—Lee Edwards, author and editor, describing his first meeting with Reagan

"We talked about law enforcement and crime control, the things I had spent the last ten years working on. I was amazed.... He seemed to know as much as I did. After a while, he offered me the job and I accepted on the spot. I drove home and told my wife we were moving to Sacramento." —Edwin Meese, U.S. attorney general and chief of staff to the governor

As California's first lady, Nancy Reagan had several projects of her own, such as the Foster Grandparents program. At left, she bids good-bye to a group of Republican women outside the governor's mansion in 1967. The 1877 house oozed charm, but it was also dilapidated and a firetrap. Later that year, the family moved to a house in Sacramento's suburbs.

HIS VALUES "He always took the time to carefully go through the mail that came to him.... I think this came from his Hollywood days. In those days, fan mail was very important. He saw a parallel in these letters to the governor. Indeed, these were the people who had put him in office." —Nancy Clark Reynolds, special assistant to the governor

The Reagans greet Vietnam War prisoners at a homecoming reception. They gave four dinners for POWs returning to California. "Their stories were so harrowing, we wondered how they survived," Mrs. Reagan said.

HIS VISION "When I was prisoner-of-war, the Vietnamese went to great lengths to restrict the news from home to the statements and activities of prominent opponents to the war. They wanted us to believe that America

DAYS OF RAGE

Had Ronald Reagan set out to enter politics in the most strife-ridden, conflicted, discordant decade in the twentieth century, he could not have done better than the 1960s. There were times in that ten-year span when the nation seemed bent on tearing itself apart, quaking along a deep fault line that divided the generations.

The United States' growing commitment to the Vietnam War was costing so many young lives (some twenty-five thousand had been killed by the end of 1967), and Americans who thought the war pointless and unjust—most of them young themselves—were defying the draft and taking to the streets in protest. In the turmoil, there seemed to be no middle ground, no room for civil discourse. The generation that had fought World War II largely regarded the young antiwar activists as ungrateful, unpatriotic cowards; the dissenters dismissed their elders as warmongering hypocrites.

Throughout the country, college campuses were hotbeds of dissent against the war, and against the establishment in general. This was particularly true in California, where the renowned University of California system was virtually under siege. In the course of one year, there were eight bombings or attempted bombings on the Berkeley campus alone, and police confiscated nearly a thousand sticks of dynamite and more than two hundred firearms.

A focal point for the fury was Governor Ronald Reagan. Students who before his election had cheered him because he was not part of the establishment now burned him in effigy, and his public appearances were greeted with obscene taunts and jeers from young protesters. Not only was he now part of the establishment but he also supported the war. Reagan believed the fight in Southeast Asia was necessary to prevent a communist takeover of the entire region. His own dissent was against an administration he felt was hobbling America's military, directing it to fight a war without giving it the wherewithal to win.

His own views notwithstanding, he conceded the good intentions of some of the students and their right to protest. He had, however, no patience with their methods. "The upheaval that shook so many of our campuses when I was governor wasn't a gallant or idealistic rebellion to right some wrongs," he said. "It was violent anarchy."

A photo from Nancy Reagan's private collection shows the governor greeting a group of children following a reception for the POWs. At the bottom of the picture Reagan had written, "May it never happen to them."

had forgotten us. They never mentioned Ronald Reagan to us, or played his speeches over the camp loudspeakers. No matter. We knew about him. New additions to our ranks told us how Governor and Mrs. Reagan were committed to our liberation and our cause." —John McCain, senator from Arizona

He decided to deal first with college administrators who refused to discipline the rioters: Early in 1967, he oversaw the firing of the president of the state's University of California system. He then turned to the dissenters themselves, trying to engage them in dialogue, but the radicalism only increased.

The tumult approached its apogee in 1968. In January, the North Vietnamese unleashed the Tet offensive, an onslaught that eventually brought more than a million more South Vietnamese under communist control. Desperate to force the enemy into serious peace talks, President Lyndon Johnson's administration responded by escalating America's participation in the war. The subsequent antiwar outcry was enough to effectively force Johnson from office: In March, he announced he would not seek another term. In June, Senator Robert F. Kennedy, running for president on an antiwar platform, was assassinated in Los Angeles, further inflaming antiwar sentiment. And in the spring of 1969, some two thousand rioters charged a line of police in Berkeley, injuring forty-seven.

As Reagan saw it, a minority of spoiled, elitist kids disdainful of the privilege of attending the state's fine

Governor Reagan fields questions in a press conference, circa 1973. At his left is Commander Richard Stratton, a prisoner of war who had just returned home to California from Vietnam.

universities was making it impossible for the majority of students to get an education. After the 1969 assault on the police at Berkeley, he called in the National Guard, and calm began returning to California's campuses.

Liberals would never forgive him for his hard-line stand. But vast numbers of Americans who agreed with him would never forget it.

Americans who had been prisoners of war would certainly remember. Their captors had allowed them to hear only news of dissent at home, but word of Ronald Reagan's stand had traveled along Hanoi's prison grapevines and bolstered their hope and courage. Vietnam veterans returning home not to a heroes' welcome but to derision and contempt would remember that Ronald Reagan had stood up for them and honored their sacrifice.

So would the millions of ordinary Americans who simply loved their country and were aghast at a counterculture that seemed bent on trashing it, and them. They were middle class and working class, Republicans and Democrats. They would take note that at least one man had stood up to the radicals, and they, too, would remember.

HIS VALUES *"Ronnie could not and would not condone the students' violence or give in to force. He felt education provided by the state was a privilege, and the price you paid for it was decent behavior, respect for others, and hard work. Sadly, he lost the youth for a while. I think that bothered him almost more than anything else during his time as governor."* —Nancy Reagan

"Lawlessness by the mob, as with the individual, will not be tolerated. We will act firmly and quickly to put down riot or insurrection wherever and whenever the situation requires."

—Ronald Reagan, in his first inaugural address as governor, 1967

Demonstrators gather in People's Park at UC-Berkeley while police watch from behind a mesh fence. The installation of the fence on May 15, 1969—built to keep hippies out of the park—ignited a riot in which one protester was killed by police. Days later, Reagan called in the National Guard.

On to bigger things, Ron and Nancy hit the presidential campaign trail in early 1976. Reagan chose Senator Richard Schweicker from Pennslyvania, a friend and like-minded conservative, as his running mate.

HIS VOICE "A candidate doesn't make the decision to run for president; the people make it for him." —Ronald Reagan

THE SPIRIT OF '76

Easily reelected California's governor in 1970, Ronald Reagan had broad support to seek a third term four years later. But he declined. He had achieved the main goal of his second term, welfare reform, and at sixty-five, he was looking forward to the pleasures of private citizenship.

But throughout the country, voices were calling him away—and he could not turn a deaf ear. He was concerned about the federal government's relentless expansion, its profligate squandering of funds and lives. In November 1975, he announced his intention to run.

His opponent for the Republican nomination would be President Gerald Ford, who had succeeded Richard Nixon in 1974 when Nixon resigned in the wake of the Watergate scandal. Reagan disliked opposing a Republican incumbent, but felt that Ford—the only president in America's history not elected by the people—was vulnerable.

From the outset Reagan was the front-runner, but in the crucial first primary he left New Hampshire two days before the vote to campaign in Illinois. Feeling taken for granted, New Hampshire voters gave Ford a narrow victory, and with that momentum Ford won the next four primaries.

Reagan's campaign was broke, and major Republican officeholders were calling on him, in the name of party unity, to drop out. He refused. Rallying, he won North Carolina, Texas, Georgia, Alabama, and Indiana.

By the time the Republican National Convention convened in August, Ford had only a slight edge in delegates. But the power of the incumbency and the party apparatus made the difference. Ford won the nomination, 1,187 to 1,070. Reagan appeared at the convention on the final night to a thunderous welcome, and after Ford gave his acceptance speech, he invited Ron and Nancy to join him on the podium. Reagan gave an impromptu six-minute speech, calling for the party to unify and "communicate to the world that we may be fewer in numbers than we've ever been but we carry the message they're waiting for."

The audience's response was startling: Delegates who had stood to honor him remained standing the entire time he spoke—something no one remembered ever happening before—and at the end their applause was louder and longer than it had been for their own nominee.

Ronald Reagan was not sure that night whether he would run again in four years, but one thing appeared certain: He would be asked.

Reagan takes a break from the campaign trail in June 1976. The race for the nomination was tight, but he refused to attack Gerald Ford, vowing not to commit what he called "the Eleventh Commandment": speaking ill of another Republican.

"Of Ronnie's five campaigns for public office, the one I remember most vividly is the only one he lost. That was in 1976, when he challenged President Gerald Ford for the Republican nomination. That campaign was so exciting, so dramatic, and so emotional—especially at the convention—that in my mind it almost overshadowed Ronnie's four victories." —Nancy Reagan

The Reagans unwind on their campaign plane in August 1976. After their narrow loss at the convention, Nancy Reagan would remember, "I was really disappointed that Ronnie didn't get the nomination. I couldn't keep the tears from streaming down my face while he spoke. But in the end, everything turned out for the best. As Ronnie would say, God had a plan. Four years later, we would find out what it was."

HIS VOICE "It was a political fantasy. In less than six minutes the man whom the delegates rejected only twenty-four hours before now inspired them and united them. A few delegates were to later

Reagan waves to delegates, at left, on the last night of the 1976 convention. Joining in the deafening applause are Nelson Rockefeller, Gerald Ford, Betty Ford, and vice presidential nominee Robert Dole. Reagan and Vice President Nelson Rockefeller join their party's nominee, incumbent president Gerald Ford (above) on the podium at the Republican National Convention in Kansas City on August 18, 1976.

admit that as he spoke, they began to have second thoughts. 'We may have picked the wrong man,' one said." —Martin Anderson, domestic and economic policy adviser, scholar, and author

The Reagans make their exit from the 1976 GOP convention. Reagan's race for the presidential nomination that year was the only one he ever lost.

HIS VISION "When the convention was over and we were all preparing to leave, we first had a gathering of the campaign workers in the hotel ballroom. There was hardly a dry eye in the house. Claire [my wife] went

over to Governor Reagan and thanked him for all he had done and how he had conducted himself. He said, 'Well, Claire, you shouldn't be upset about the outcome because it wasn't part of God's plan.'" —Richard Schweiker, U.S. senator from Pennsylvania and Reagan's 1976 running mate

Part of Reagan's success came from his ability to reach across party lines and speak to all Americans. His bipartisan, no-nonsense approach inspired many Democratic moderates to become "Reagan Democrats." With their vote, he won by a landslide.

HIS VISION "Napoleon once said, 'A leader is a dealer of hope.' In the campaign of 1980 Ronald Reagan offered the American people hope. He had a vision and a plan. He promised to reduce taxes and end the growth of government and government regulation. He promised to restore

A VOICE OF HOPE

When Ronald Reagan lost to Gerald Ford in 1976, he remarked to an aide, "I'm not disappointed that I didn't get the nomination. I wasn't ready for it." It is also probable that the nation was not quite ready for him, either—or, at the time, for any Republican. The Watergate debacle had soured the electorate on Republicans, one factor that led to Ford's own defeat at the hands of Jimmy Carter.

But the Carter presidency failed to ease the gloom that seemed to settle over the nation in the 1970s. People had only begun to heal from the violent, divisive '60s and the agony of Vietnam when Watergate revealed to them lies and deceit at the highest levels of their government. Then, under Carter came an energy crisis, a looming recession, and the rare phenomenon of stagflation—stagnant economic growth and double-digit inflation occurring at the same time. Overtaxed and overregulated businesses shied away from expending capital, and individuals whose income was already being whittled away by oppressive taxes found it further decimated by skyrocketing prices.

Military spending was cut even as America's strategic

THE START OF JIMMY PEANUTS WATERLOO

DETROIT   1980

REPUBLICAN NATIONAL CONVENTION

A Republican National Committee campaign button depicts incumbent president Jimmy Carter, a former peanut farmer, as a peanut-size Napoleon.

weapons grew obsolete and morale in the armed services plunged. Abroad, the Soviet Union brought nine more countries into its sphere of influence between 1974 and 1979 and, as the decade ended, invaded Afghanistan. America, meanwhile, was humiliated in front of the entire world as the Carter administration failed to manage the release of fifty-five U.S. hostages held by terrorists in Iran for more than a year.

In July 1979, President Carter, in a nationally televised speech, discussed the "malaise" he thought was afflicting America, a "crisis of confidence" that he said was attacking "the very heart and soul and spirit of our national will."

Ronald Reagan may have agreed that the nation faced a welter of woes and that confidence was indeed lacking. But he felt it was up to America's leaders to restore it, to remind the people of their own greatness.

"I found nothing wrong with the American people," he said. "We had to recapture our dreams, our pride in ourselves and our country, and regain that unique sense of destiny and optimism that had always made America different from any other country in the world. If I could

American military strength. He promised to treat threats to American security with firmness and resolve, and he did. He approached the presidency with a sense of purpose, a vision of the public good, and the political skills needed to pursue them." —Jeane Kirkpatrick, U.S. ambassador to the United Nations and scholar

be elected president, I wanted to do what I could to bring about a spiritual revival in America. I believed that America's greatest years were ahead of it, that we had to look at the things that had made it the greatest, richest, and most progressive country on earth in the first place, decide what had gone wrong, and then put it back on course."

Reagan was certain that Americans would see no course correction under the Democrats. "After a half century that had given them the New Deal and the 'Great Society' and produced a government that took an average of 45 percent of the national wealth," he said, "people were just fed up."

What was needed, he believed, was a return to a basic idea as old as the republic itself, so old that in a cynical and disillusioned age it was once again revolutionary—the idea that the American people could be trusted to govern themselves. They were smart and industrious enough to produce and manage wealth on an unparalleled scale if the government would only get out of their pockets and off their

backs. They were kind and moral enough to help each other without looking to the government to take care of them. They were strong and resolved enough not just to contain or coexist with communism but to compete with it and ultimately conquer it. They were wise enough to regard their unique history, their legacy of freedom, and remember once again to be proud.

As Reagan pondered whether to try again for the presidency, the basics of a potential campaign were clear in his mind: a 30 percent across-the-board tax cut to jolt the economy out of the doldrums, increased military spending to assure peace through strength, and social policies affirming traditional American decency and common sense. He envisioned no quick fixes for the nation's ills, but he correctly assessed that for all their disillusionment and distress, Americans would get behind a leader who had confidence in them and in his own direction.

By 1980, America was ready for Ronald Reagan—and he was ready to be president.

NATIONAL PRIDE

★

Reagan's belief in America's greatness was genuine and unbounded. By 1980, he had seen Americans win two world wars, overcome a depression, land a man on the moon, and introduce cutting-edge technology. America is great, said Reagan, because its people are great. "Don't let anyone tell you that America's best days are behind her—that the American spirit has been vanquished," he urged in his second inaugural address. "We've seen it triumph too often in our lives to stop believing in it now." Aided by Reagan's optimism, Americans did believe—and ushered in an era of unprecedented national pride.

"In the forty years since first meeting Ronald Reagan, he has taught me a lot, not so much through words as by example. His optimistic spirit was contagious.... That attitude affected the country psychologically and won him much admiration even among his critics.... That spirit was infectious, and the nation was better for it." —Billy Graham, evangelist

HIS VALUES "It was not a false optimism. It wasn't an optimism based upon unrealistic expectations, but it was an optimism which was based upon the capabilities of the American people . . . on the values of our country." —Edwin Meese, U.S. attorney general and chief of staff to the governor

Nancy Reagan joins her husband in his 1980 run for the presidency. Though she parted from him once or twice to drum up support on his behalf, she, like most prospective first ladies, remained at his side throughout most of the campaign.

REAGAN
FOR PRESIDENT
Let's make America great again.

The time is now. Reagan

AMERICA
REAGAN COUNTRY

HIS VALUES "On the eve of his election as president in 1980, a reporter asked Reagan what it was that people saw in him. 'Would you laugh if I told you that I think, maybe, they see themselves and that I'm one of them?' he replied. 'I've never been able to detach myself or think that I, somehow, am apart from them.' These words still ring true." —Lou Cannon, journalist and Reagan biographer

"'I'm not politically ambitious,' Reagan said. 'What—not politically ambitious?' I asked in astonishment. 'You want to be president of the United States.' 'That's right, but I'm not on any ego trip or glory ride. I'm running because I think there is a job to do and I want to do it,' he said." —Mike Wallace, senior correspondent for *60 Minutes*, recalling a 1980 interview with Reagan

At his election headquarters in Los Angeles, the president-elect joins his supporters in a thumbs-up after his landslide win over Jimmy Carter. The victory was so sweeping that television networks were able to call the race on the afternoon of election day.

"*Everybody started yelling. Suddenly, I was on my feet, shouting, 'You tell him, honey, you tell him!' A moment later I caught myself and thought, Oh Lord, I hope the cameras weren't on me. Of course, the cameras were on him, and days later, it was on national news. With those seven words, Ronnie took control of his campaign. It was the turning point.*" —Nancy Reagan, reflecting on the New Hampshire debate

THE GREAT DEBATES

Sometimes political fates can hang on a few well-chosen words delivered in the right way at the right time. So it was in Ronald Reagan's 1980 bid for the presidency. When he entered the race for the Republican nomination, the field was crowded. It was important to each candidate to distinguish himself in the New Hampshire primary. Thus, a televised debate sponsored by a local newspaper, the *Nashua Telegraph,* took on considerable weight.

The paper intended to involve only the two top candidates, George Bush and Ronald Reagan, but Reagan thought all seven should be heard—as did they. Senator Bob Dole complained to the Federal Elections Commission that in restricting the debate, the *Telegraph* was contributing illegally to the Reagan and Bush campaigns. The FEC agreed: The paper could manage the event, but not sponsor it. In the end, Reagan decided to pay for the debate himself. Then he invited the others to participate.

The night of the debate, the candidates arrived to find only two chairs. George Bush sat uncomfortably in one while his people insisted on a two-man debate or nothing. Unable to find a compromise, Reagan and the others walked onto the stage together. He sat while they stood behind him.

The crowd grew restless, but when Reagan started to explain, the debate's moderator shouted, "Mr. Reagan is out of order. Turn his microphone off." Coolly but emphatically, Reagan said, "I *paid* for this microphone, Mr. Green."

The man's name was *Breen,* but the crowd didn't mind. They roared their approval at Reagan's firm fair-mindedness, and the debate went on. "I may have won the debate, the primary—and the nomination—right there," Reagan would assess. He arrived months later at the national convention the predetermined nominee.

In the general election, the Democrats labored to portray him as a coldhearted, trigger-happy, right-wing extremist, but that could not penetrate his armor of affability. In a televised debate on October 28, President Carter began accusing Reagan of hostility toward Medicare. With a genial smile, the Republican nominee shook his head with grandfatherly exasperation and said, "There you go again." The image was indelible, as was his question to the American people: "Are you better off than you were four years ago?"

They evidently thought not. On November 4, Ronald Reagan was elected fortieth president of the United States in a landslide.

HIS VOICE "Well, for some reason my words hit the audience, whose emotions were already worked up, like a sledgehammer. The crowd roared and just went wild."

—Ronald Reagan, reflecting on the New Hampshire debate

"[A] recession is when your neighbor loses his job. A depression is when you lose yours. And recovery is when Jimmy Carter loses his!"

—Ronald Reagan, on the 1980 campaign trail

HIS VISION "Our oldest president was really the Great Rejuvenator. Ronald Reagan made America feel young again, with its mission in history uncompleted and its greatest accomplishments yet to come." —Adam Meyerson, editor of *Policy Review*

The Reagans greet an enthusiastic crowd, above, in South Carolina in October 1980. At left, Reagan supporters cheer their nominee wildly at a 1980 campaign rally, making it clear that they were ready for a change in the White House.

"Ronnie never sought higher office on his own, but rather as an answer to the party's call for unity and someone to lead." —Nancy Reagan

A triumphant-looking Ronald Reagan energizes hundreds of supporters in a late-1980 campaign rally. He was the first actor ever to be elected president.

"A few minutes after five, I took a bath and Ronnie went into the shower. We had the television on very loud in our bedroom so we could hear the news. Suddenly, I heard . . . that Ronnie was going to win in a landslide victory. I leaped out of the tub, threw a towel around me, and started banging on the

shower door. Ronnie got out, grabbed a towel, and we ran over to the television set. And there we stood, dripping wet as we heard that Ronnie had just been elected! I was thrilled, and stunned. 'Congratulations, honey,' I said, as I hugged the fortieth president of the United States."

—Nancy Reagan, recalling election night, 1980

A Voice for America

"America's best days

Shortly after Ronald Reagan's inauguration, House Speaker Tip O'Neill informed him, "You're in the big leagues now." The remark was rather condescending, as it came from the country's most powerful Democrat. It also carried an implicit message: The newcomer may have come to town with revolutionary plans for change, but the old hands would teach him how things really worked in Washington.

Reagan, however, would soon leave O'Neill—and doubtless many other veteran politicians—breathless at his own political skill. Six months into his first term, the president made good on his central campaign promise by signing into law the biggest tax cut in American history. In maneuvering the measure through the Senate and particularly through the House, where O'Neill's Democrats were in the majority, he had pulled off what the *Washington Post's* David Broder called "one of the most remarkable demonstrations of presidential leadership in modern history."

It was then that even his critics began to suspect that Reagan just might be in a league of his own.

He had made America promises he meant to keep. And against all odds—against strong opposition from his detractors and sometimes even his friends, against an assassin's bullet that came within millimeters of killing him—he would keep his promises.

are yet to come."

He had told the nation that the revolution he intended to lead would not be easy. Progress would be slow, he said, "measured in inches and feet, not miles." But there would be progress. At first it was hard to detect any forward movement. Even as Reagan began putting forth his agenda, cutting taxes and rebuilding the military, the nation sank into a deep recession—the worst economic slowdown since the Great Depression. Businesses closed their doors, farms faced foreclosure, people lost their jobs. Only two years into his first term, Reagan seemed doomed to oversee a failed presidency. His critics charged that he was leading the nation toward disaster; as his popularity plummeted, even his allies grew alarmed. Many urged him to turn back. He would not. "Stay the course" became his watchword; give his program time to work. And though national patience wore thin, it did not wear out. America did stay the course, and the result was an era of unparalleled prosperity. Reagan had promised to cut taxes, curb inflation, lower interest rates, and cut unemployment. He did all those things. He had promised an economic recovery. He produced an economic boom.

He had also promised to restore respect for America abroad. Here, too, his efforts would stir up controversy. When in 1983 he called the Soviet Union an "evil empire," there was an outcry that he was unraveling previous administrations' progress toward détente, which for years had kept the world's two superpowers poised in uneasy peace. When that same year he announced plans for his Strategic Defense Initiative (SDI)—a high-tech satellite system aimed at destroying any nuclear missiles an enemy might launch—the media derisively dubbed it "Star Wars" and critics predicted it would escalate the arms race. And when, months later, he sent American troops to counter a communist threat on the tiny Caribbean island of Grenada, opponents charged that he was presenting America as an international bully.

But Reagan knew who the real bully was, and his strategy for stopping him was clearer and more farsighted than anyone imagined. In fact, the ultimate outcome would be more sweeping and complete than he probably imagined himself: The long and costly Cold War would end, and the victory would vindicate not only Reagan's vision but democratic government itself.

As his first term drew to an end, this momentous development still lay in the future. Even so, he could look back in 1984 and ask Americans a familiar question—"Are you better off than you were four years ago?"—confident that this time, most would answer yes.

HIS VISION "It is time for us to realize that we're too great a nation to limit ourselves to small dreams. . . . Let us begin an era of national renewal. Let us renew our determination, our courage, and our strength. And let us renew our faith and our hope. . . . The crisis we are facing today . . . [requires] our best effort and our willingness to believe in ourselves and to believe in

"our capacity to perform great deeds; to believe that together with God's help we can and will resolve the problems which now confront us. And after all, why shouldn't we believe that? We are Americans."

—Ronald Reagan, in his first inaugural address as president, January 20, 1981

President Reagan attends to business in the Oval Office. As president he kept to a precise written schedule every day, checking off each meeting or engagement as he finished it. He was invariably punctual; he hated to keep people waiting.

Chief Justice Warren Burger administers the oath of office to the new president at Reagan's inauguration on January 20, 1981. Mrs. Reagan stands beside her husband. Behind her is Senator Mark Hatfield, chairman of the Joint Congressional Committee on Inaugural Ceremonies.

"As he raised his head to look out at the crowd, a strange and wonderful thing happened. The dark cloudy sky over his head began to part slightly, within seconds there was a gaping hole in the gray overcast, and a brilliant, golden shaft of wintry sun burst through the clouds and bathed the inaugural stand

A NEW BEGINNING

Despite the dreary January weather, there was a spring-like air in the inauguration of the fortieth president of the United States, a feeling of renewal. Ronald Reagan was, at sixty-nine, the oldest man ever to take the presidential oath. Even so, he looked fit and vigorous in his club coat, striped pants, and gray vest.

For the first time, the swearing-in ceremony took place on the steps of the west front of the Capitol, with its heart-stopping view of the Mall, the Washington Monument, and the Lincoln Memorial.

Chief Justice Warren Burger administered the oath of office first to the new vice president, George Bush. Then, a little before noon, Reagan took his place on the podium. His wife was at his side, dressed in red. In her hands was Nelle Reagan's much-loved Bible—old, crumbling, and held together with tape. As Nancy Reagan held it out for her husband to rest his left hand on it, it lay open to Second Chronicles, chapter seven, verse fourteen:

"If my people, which are called by my name, shall humble themselves, and pray, and seek my face, and turn from their wicked ways; then will I hear from heaven, and will forgive their sin, and will heal their land." Beside these words Nelle had written, "A most wonderful verse for the healing of the nations."

As Reagan swore to preserve, protect, and defend the constitution of the United States, it must have seemed to many that God was indeed listening: The clouds suddenly parted, and golden light shone on the podium. The effect was magical.

"What was even more amazing was that the same kind of thing had happened in Sacramento during Ronnie's first inauguration as governor," Nancy Reagan would recall. "It had been a cold, drizzly, and overcast day, but when Ronnie got up to speak, the sun came out. When it happened again this time, I was overcome with joy."

The sun continued shining as Reagan gave his inaugural address: "The economic ills we suffer have come upon us over several decades," he said. "They will not go away in days, weeks or months, but they will go away. They will go away because we as Americans have the capacity now, as we've had in the past, to do whatever needs to be done to preserve this last and greatest bastion of freedom."

As he finished, the clouds closed in. It was over—and just beginning.

"It all felt unreal. Could it really be that Ronald Reagan, my husband, was about to become fortieth president of the United States? How did this ever happen? It was like a dream."
—Nancy Reagan

and the watching crowd. As Reagan spoke, a slight breeze ruffled his hair and the warm golden light beamed down on him. Later, a few minutes after he finished speaking, as if on cue from some master lighter backstage, the hole in the clouds shrank, the sky darkened, and Washington grew gray and cold once again." —Martin Anderson, domestic and economic policy adviser, scholar, and author

The Reagans wave to well-wishers during the inaugural parade. The parade, which proceeded down Pennsylvania Avenue from the Capitol to the White House, included a high school marching band from Dixon, Illinois, the president's childhood hometown.

HIS VALUES "As we passed the crowds, people cheered and clapped and I wore out my arms waving back to them.... That evening I wrote in my diary: 'I keep thinking this can't continue and yet their warmth and affection seems so genuine I get a lump in my throat. I pray constantly that I won't let them down.'" —Ronald Reagan

The Presidential Inaugural Committee requests the honor of your presence to attend and participate in the Inauguration of

Ronald Wilson Reagan as President of the United States of America and *George Herbert Walker Bush* as Vice President of the United States of America on Tuesday the twentieth of January one thousand nine hundred and eighty-one in the City of Washington

The Reagan family gathers in the White House, above, for an inauguration night portrait. Later in the evening, the president and first lady managed to attend all ten inaugural balls in a brief four hours. The festivities didn't stop there, however. Much of the president and first lady's time would be spent hosting and attending fund-raisers, dinners, and other galas. The Reagans wait at left to be shuttled to another event in late February 1981.

"For so long, I had shared the reverence most Americans have for that historic building; back when I was a kid in Dixon, I'd imagined what the private part of the White House must be like, but I had never imagined myself actually living there. Now, we had gone in the front door, gotten on an elevator, and we were here to stay—at least for four years. If I could do this, I thought, then truly any child in America had an opportunity to do it." —Ronald Reagan

A dollar bill illustrates the theme of President Reagan's televised address to the nation, which he drafted himself, on February 5, 1981. He spoke about the troubled economy and the measures he thought necessary to set it right.

"We had seven and a half years of sustained, noninflationary growth; we took six million poor Americans off the tax rolls; it was the longest peacetime expansion in the history of this country. Why? Because of supply-side economics." —James Baker, chief of staff and secretary of the treasury

STAYING THE COURSE

Several economic theorists have claimed credit for the prosperity that came to be associated with Ronald Reagan's presidency. But Reagan acknowledged that his primary—and rather unlikely—influence had been Hollywood. There, he had been in the 91 percent tax bracket, and had quickly learned how little incentive there was to work more for only nine cents on the dollar. He'd also found that when people like him worked less, fewer film jobs were available. From this he drew certain conclusions.

"Any system that penalizes success and accomplishment is wrong," he said. "If, on the other hand, you reduce tax rates and allow people to spend or save more of what they earn, they'll be more industrious; they'll have more incentive to work hard, and money they earn will add fuel to the great economic machine that energizes our national progress. The result: more prosperity for all—and more revenue for government. A few economists call this principle supply-side economics," he said. "I just call it common sense."

In 1981, Reagan pushed through Congress a historic tax package that featured a 25 percent across-the-board reduction over three years. He also began rebuilding the military. Yet the immediate result was hardly prosperity for all. The economy, already troubled when he took office, nosedived. Unemployment soared: some ten million Americans were jobless. Industry and farming suffered, and the number of people living in poverty rose to 15 percent. Pundits tagged his theory "Reaganomics" and cried that it was proving an economic wrecking ball. The president's popularity fell to 35 percent, but he would not abandon his policy.

"Stay the course" became his mantra as he called on Americans to endure and hope. By 1983, when his last tax cut took effect, the economy had turned the corner, beginning a seven-year growth period that the *Wall Street Journal* called "the biggest peacetime economic boom in U.S. history."

Reagan knew he had been vindicated and quipped, "The best sign that our economic program is working is that they don't call it Reaganomics anymore."

President Reagan delivers a body blow to 12 percent inflation as he valiantly aims to take it down to 3 percent in this April 1982 Brooks cartoon from the *Birmingham News*.

"'Stay the course' was an attempt to confer dignity to struggle. It was a message of hope because it reaffirmed to the people that there was a course.... And it asked of the American people endurance, in the expectation that the situation was going to improve."

—Dinesh D'Souza, author, scholar, and Reagan biographer

GRACE UNDER FIRE

A little over three months after taking office, Ronald Reagan was leaving the Washington Hilton Hotel after a speech. Nearing his limousine, he heard to his left a series of popping noises. They sounded like firecrackers. The next thing the president knew, he was being thrown inside the car by Secret Service agent Jerry Parr. "I landed on my face atop the armrest across the backseat and Jerry jumped on top of me," Reagan would report. "When he landed, I felt a pain in my upper back that was unbelievable. It was the most excruciating pain I had ever felt."

He thought Parr had broken one of his ribs. In fact, the president had been shot. Parr ordered the driver to head for the White House, then saw bright blood bubbling from Reagan's mouth. He called out to head for George Washington University Hospital instead.

At the emergency entrance the president made his way out of the car and took a few steps before he felt his legs give way. He was wheeled inside on a gurney and almost instantly surrounded by doctors. Providentially, most of the hospital's physicians had been attending a

Secret Service agents and police protect the president as he leaves the Washington Hilton on March 30, 1981. Moments later, Reagan would be fighting for his life, shot by a would-be assassin.

conference, and a host of specialists were on hand. One of them told Reagan they would have to operate.

"I hope you're a Republican," the president quipped.

"Today, Mr. President, we're all Republicans," the doctor said.

It was while he was in the emergency room that Reagan began learning what had happened at the Washington Hilton. A troubled young man named John Hinckley, Jr., had tried to assassinate him. In the process, Hinckley had shot and gravely wounded Press Secretary Jim Brady. Secret Service agent Tim McCarthy had been hit in the chest and Washington police officer Tom Delehanty in the neck. Hinckley had been wrestled to the ground and taken into custody.

Surgeons would discover that Reagan's own wound had come close to killing him. He had been hit just as Parr was flinging him into the car. The bullet had careened off the limousine and through the gap between the car and its opened door. Flattened into a sharp disk, it had sliced into Reagan under his left arm, hit a rib, and torn into his left lung, stopping less than an inch from his heart. Doctors said

"I was so shaken by the events of that spring that it took me a couple of years just to say the word 'shooting.' For a long time I simply referred to it as 'March 30,' or, even more obliquely, as 'the thing that happened to Ronnie.' For me, the entire episode was, quite literally, unspeakable." —Nancy Reagan

GET WELL SOON!
Mr. President
Jim, Tim, and Tom

HIS VALUES "When I was lying there in the hospital, looking up at the ceiling and wondering if I was going to die, I spent a lot of time praying, and I knew I couldn't just pray for myself. I had to pray for John Hinckley, too. And if God loves me, then in spite of everything, He must also love John Hinckley." —Ronald Reagan, reflecting on his would-be assassin

White House staffers gather on the steps of the Old Executive Office Building to wish a quick recovery to the president and the others wounded in the shooting at the Hilton: Press Secretary Jim Brady, Secret Service agent Tim McCarthy, and Washington policeman Tom Delehanty. All would survive.

The Reagans return to the White House on April 11, 1981, after the president is released from George Washington University Hospital. Reagan was the first American president ever to survive being wounded in an assassination attempt while in office.

"You have suffered the passion of the cross and received grace. There is a purpose to this. Because of your suffering and pain you will now understand the suffering and pain of the world. This has happened to you at this time because your country and the world need you."

—Mother Teresa to Ronald Reagan after the attempted assassination

that had he arrived at the hospital scant minutes later, he probably would have died.

As news of the assassination attempt flashed across the world, there was confusion, alarm, dread, and finally relief and an outpouring of admiration and affection for the president's extraordinary courage.

At first the reports said that he had not been hit. It was only after his clothes had been cut away that doctors found the small but potentially lethal wound. By that time, Nancy Reagan had arrived, breathless, at the hospital.

There she found bedlam—doctors and nurses shouting, laboring to help the president. Unable to see her husband as doctors worked to save him, she could only wait and pray. "Nurses kept coming in with new reports," she said, "and the news they brought was increasingly alarming. Twice I was told that they couldn't find Ronnie's pulse. They were afraid he might go into shock. If that happened, I knew we might lose him."

Yet it was Reagan himself who, in moments of consciousness, managed to hearten his wife and the nation. When Nancy was first allowed at his bedside just before his operation, he pushed up his oxygen mask and his blood-caked lips man-

One of the many walking sticks President Reagan received as a gesture of good will and good humor after the attempted assassination

aged a smile. Borrowing Jack Dempsey's line to his wife after losing the heavyweight championship, he whispered: "Honey, I forgot to duck."

The surgery was long and arduous. Doctors had trouble locating the bullet, and there was the constant threat of shock from blood loss. Almost all the president's blood had to be replaced. But he came through it, and throughout his recuperation continued to show that brave and reassuring humor that convinced the world that his spirit was intact, that he was on the mend.

Waking up in the recovery room, unable to speak, he wrote a note to his doctors: "All in all, I'd rather be in Philadelphia." And later, "Can we rewrite this scene beginning at the time I left the hotel?" and "Send me to L.A., where I can see the air I'm breathing!"

Beneath the humor, though, the president would gain from his ordeal a deepened spirituality. Everything—even the attempted assassination—happened for a purpose, he believed. Mercifully, his life had been spared. "Whatever happens now," he reflected in his journal, "I owe my life to God and will try to serve Him in every way I can."

"In his first weeks in office, Reagan demonstrated repeatedly a kind of personal ease and charm that not only delighted his audience but disarmed his critics.…When he displayed that same wit and grace in the hours after his own life was threatened, he elevated those appealing qualities to the level of legend." —David Broder of the *Washington Post*

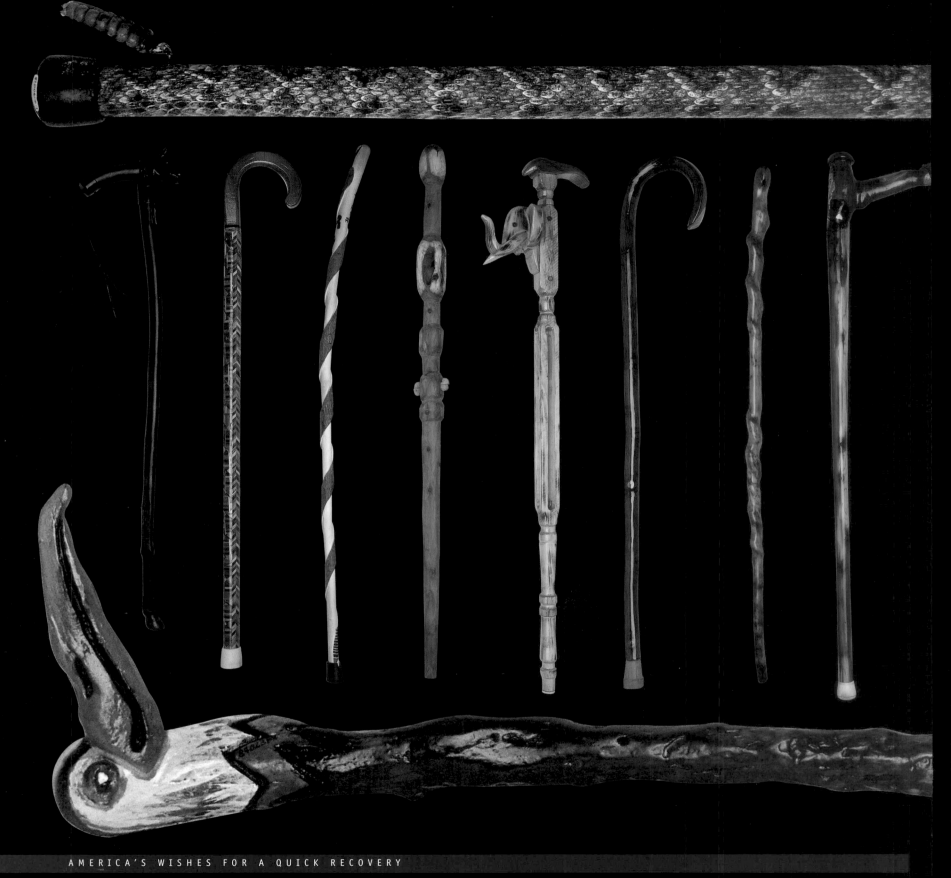

HIS VALUES *"Most men or women, when they get married, like to feel that their husband or wife, if put to the test, if put under tremendous pressure, would act in a certain way, would act with great strength and make you very proud of them. You like to feel that. But very seldom does the average person have a chance to really see that husband or wife under those kinds of circumstances. I've been very lucky in that,*

because I've seen my husband under very pressured conditions. I know he's never failed. Never failed me. He's always stuck to principles. He's never done anything for purely political reasons. You go back to the assassination attempt. I don't know of many men who would have handled it that well." —Nancy Reagan

Following the shooting, thousands of Americans sent sympathy cards, their assurance of prayer, and over fifty walking sticks, now preserved at the Ronald Reagan Presidential Library.

Speaking to clergymen meeting in Orlando, Florida, Reagan calls the Soviet Union "the evil empire." Critics decried the phrase as reckless rhetoric, but the president said he used it "with malice aforethought; I wanted to remind the Soviets we knew what they were up to."

HIS VISION "President Reagan's Strategic Defence Initiative, about which the Soviets and Mr. Gorbachev were already so alarmed, was to prove central to the West's victory in the Cold War. . . . Looking back, it is now clear to me that Ronald Reagan's original decision on SDI was the single most important of his presidency." —Margaret Thatcher, prime minister of Great Britain

THE EVIL EMPIRE

Ronald Reagan viewed the Cold War as a basic battle—one between right and wrong: Democracy represented what was best in humanity, communism what was worst. Thus communism was inherently evil, he believed, and said so. In a speech to the National Association of Evangelicals on March 8, 1983, Reagan famously referred to the Soviet Union as "the evil empire" and called it "the focus of evil in the modern world." His words created a firestorm of controversy, for in asserting the moral superiority of the free world, he was signaling a fundamental change in foreign policy.

Since the end of World War II, America had maintained a queasy equilibrium between itself and the Soviet Union, the two powers with the nuclear capacity to obliterate each other—and the world. Mutual assured destruction (MAD) seemed to dictate coexisting with communism as the price for avoiding global holocaust. "Containment," the watchword of American policy, aimed to limit communism's spread without confrontation and to reduce nuclear arsenals, or at least retard their growth. There was no talk of eliminating

This letter from Reagan to Yuri Andropov, general secretary of the USSR, was an early attempt to introduce nuclear discussions with the Soviet Union.

the Soviet empire, seen as an immutable fixture.

Reagan thought otherwise. He believed the USSR vulnerable at its core, its precarious economy constantly hemorrhaging money to maintain its military. "The Russians could never win the arms race," he said. "We could outspend them forever"—and thus force them to their knees.

The president also believed that MAD was as insane as its acronym implied: He did not want to reduce nuclear weapons but to render them useless. Talks with scientists over the years had convinced him it was possible, and on March 23, 1983, he announced his Strategic Defense Initiative, an effort to implement a satellite-based system that would destroy enemy missiles before they could reach their targets.

Critics called it fantasy, claiming SDI threatened the delicate balance of terror between the superpowers. But if many Americans believed SDI was not feasible, the Soviets feared it was. They tried to persuade Reagan to abandon the plan. He would not. And history would prove him right: His stand on SDI is widely regarded as the lever that toppled the evil empire.

"Star Wars was a carefully thought out proposal, developed over many years, with the advice and consultation of some of the best nuclear weapons experts in the world. Reagan saw it as a moral alternative to mutually assured destruction; . . . [it] fundamentally changed how we in America and most of the world think about national defense." —Martin Anderson, domestic and economic policy adviser, scholar, and author

FREEDOM IN THE BALANCE

While one prong of Ronald Reagan's new foreign policy aimed to outmaneuver the Soviets diplomatically, another worked to demonstrate that they could no longer extend their empire through force of arms. The opportunity for such a demonstration arose on October 23, 1983, when the Organization of Eastern Caribbean States asked Reagan to help thwart a planned Soviet invasion of the tiny island nation of Grenada.

Grenada, which had been under local communist rule since 1979, was small but strategically located, a pivotal point for Cuba's Marxist government to support the like-minded Sandinista regime in Nicaragua. Several thousand Cubans were on the island, some engaged in building a runway that could accommodate Cuban and Soviet warplanes. The situation threatened neighboring islands as well as the Central American mainland. Moreover, about a thousand Americans lived there, most of them students at St. George's Medical College.

Reagan acted quickly. On October 25, some two thousand U.S. troops along with soldiers from several Caribbean nations stormed Grenada in a rescue mission called Operation Urgent Fury. They were met by local Marxist forces, aided by Cuban "construction workers" who turned out to be conspicuously well armed. In three days of fighting, nineteen American soldiers were killed and about a hundred more injured, but the United States won, ousting the communist government and preparing the way for free elections.

The first couple extends their support to some of the Marines injured in the Beirut bombing only several weeks before. Reagan called the Beirut and Grenada incidents "closely related."

Instead of celebration, however, the victory brought only criticism from Reagan's opponents in Congress. Dismissing the idea that Grenada belonged to the Soviet bloc or that Americans there had been in danger, they accused the president of violating a weaker nation's sovereignty. Some called on Reagan to resign; others wanted him impeached for violating international law.

But Reagan's position was bolstered when troops on Grenada uncovered large stockpiles of weapons, along with plans for making the island a Soviet military base—and contingency plans for kidnapping the American medical students. The small operation also held symbolic importance: For the first time since World War II, military action had reversed the communist takeover of a country; and for the first time since Vietnam, America had fought a military engagement abroad and won.

HIS VALUES "It was a big message to the Soviets. In fact, it was noticed all over the world. ... It showed that this was a person who was willing to take action—and was willing to take action with lots of people opposed—if he thought it was the right thing to do. And he used force. It raised the credibility of the U.S." —George P. Shultz, secretary of state

"He was the best commander in chief I ever served. He clearly supported the military. There is no doubt that the president made the decision to go into Grenada. Once he made it, that was it."

—Joseph Metcalf III, vice admiral, U.S. Navy; commander of the Grenada Invasion Force; deputy chief of naval operations

White House aides gather with President Reagan on October 23, 1983, to discuss the implications of sending troops into Beirut and other countries under threat. The next day, Reagan launched Operation Urgent Fury, which deployed thousands of U.S. troops into Grenada.

The Reagans enjoy a laugh together at their California ranch in this 1966 photo taken by Harry Benson, during their first years as governor and first lady.

HIS VOICE "I guess the most special thing of all was the humor. It was like Lincoln: Those who knew him and were asked what he was like would start to smile, and the smile was because of the funny thing he'd told them that they couldn't forget."

—Peggy Noonan, author and Reagan speechwriter

A LEGACY OF HUMOR

Much of Ronald Reagan's charm—and effectiveness—lay in his wit: not just his ability to tell a good story or deliver a one-liner, but in his deep understanding of humor's many functions. With the right yarn or phrase he could make people comfortable, break the ice, clarify a point. Some wit slices; Reagan's soothed. It was usually gentle, and when it was barbed, the darts were usually aimed at himself, self-deprecating sallies that blunted criticism and invited warmth.

He seemed almost to enjoy turning into self-parody the frequent media criticisms (usually fallacious) that he was too old for the presidency, too lazy, or intellectually lacking. When a reporter once asked him about his "short attention span," Reagan wasn't fazed. "I was going to reply to that," he said impishly, "but what the hell, let's move on to something else." And though he had never been known to nap in a cabinet meeting, he quipped that after he left office, his cabinet chair would be labeled, "Ronald Reagan Slept Here."

One day, aide Michael Deaver found the president trying to train his dog Lucky in the Oval Office. "Watch out," Deaver warned, "he's going to pee all over your desk."

"Why not?" Reagan replied. "Everyone else does."

The remark was telling, as well as funny: Reagan

The president often doodled during meetings. The habit struck some as a sign of inattentiveness, but in fact it seemed to help him concentrate.

could afford to be amused by his critics. He knew they were usually wrong and he was usually right, and he knew the American people knew it. Besides, he had learned that being underestimated was often advantageous.

As such, his humor was often strategic. At the Washington summit with Mikhail Gorbachev in 1985, the Soviet leader began a meeting on nuclear arms reduction with what Reagan Chief of Staff Howard Baker called a "machine gun-like presentation of his points." Reagan listened. Tension mounted. Then the president told a story:

A Russian and an American were arguing about the relative merits of their nations, Reagan related. "The American said, 'Look, in my country I can walk into the Oval Office and I can pound on the president's desk and say, "Mr. President, I don't like the way you are running the country,"' to which the Russian replied, 'I can do that, too.'

The American said, 'You can?' and his friend said: 'Sure. I can go into the Kremlin and pound on the general secretary's desk and say, "Mr. General Secretary, I don't like the way President Reagan is running his country."'"

Gorbachev listened solemnly, then howled with laughter. "It broke the tension," Baker said, "and then Reagan started on his agenda." It was a wonderful technique.

"He used to feed the squirrels on the White House grounds. I told him that our dogs, Millie and Ranger, had gotten into the habit of chasing squirrels and, if they caught them, did them in. Just before I became president, President Reagan had a sign made for the squirrels that he put just outside the Oval Office. It read, 'Beware of dogs.'" —George Bush, U.S. president

The newlyweds clown around, at top, during a 1954 trip to Lake Mead, Nevada. Reagan's good humor and positive outlook, as shown in the 1960s photo above, always buoyed his wife along. Later, during his White House years (bottom right), others benefited from his humor, too, as Reagan sought to delight his Oval Office staff and visitors with clever one-liners and stories.

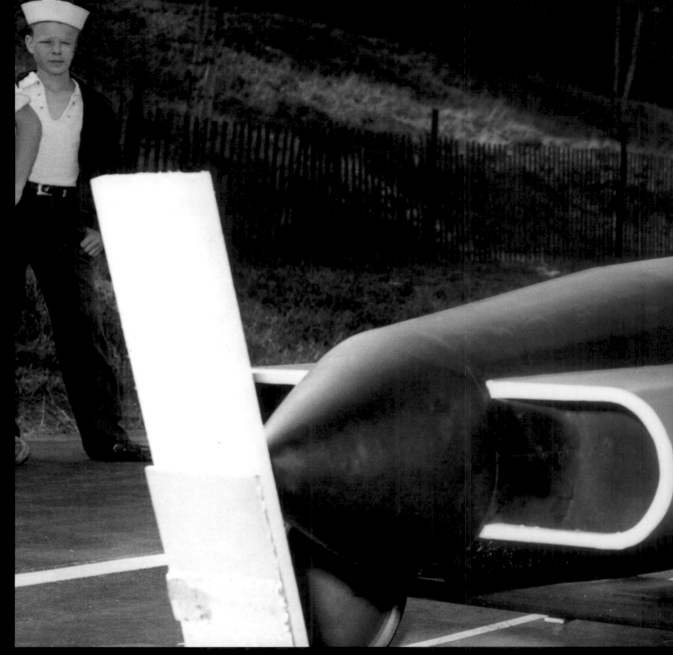

"I consider all proposals for government action with an open mind before voting 'no.'"

—Ronald Reagan, in one of his favorite lines as governor

"I've always thought that the common sense and wisdom of government were summed up in a sign they used to have hanging on that gigantic Hoover Dam. It said, 'Government property. Do not remove.'" —Ronald Reagan, in remarks at the annual meeting of the National Alliance of Business, September 14, 1987

Poised for action, left, Reagan participates in a soap box derby in California. Above, he laughs heartily at an incriminating photo taken of him at the 1983 White House News Photographers Dinner.

"It's true hard work never killed anybody, but I figure why take the chance."

—Ronald Reagan

Queen Elizabeth gets a chuckle out of President Reagan, left, at a 1983 state dinner in San Francisco, held in her honor. Just several days before, Queen Elizabeth, whom Reagan called "an accomplished horsewoman," and Prince Philip had joined the Reagans at their ranch in California.

An inveterate doodler himself, President Reagan loved political cartoons, even the ones that criticized him. Along with important news stories, his Office of News Summary once a week sent him a binder entitled "Friday's Follies," containing the week's political cartoons from across the nation. He looked forward to the Follies as a special treat.

"What I hope my epitaph will be with the White House correspondents, what every president's epitaph should be, is 'He gave as good as he got.' That, I think, makes for a healthy press and a healthy presidency." —Ronald Reagan, in remarks at the White House Correspondents' Association Dinner, 1988

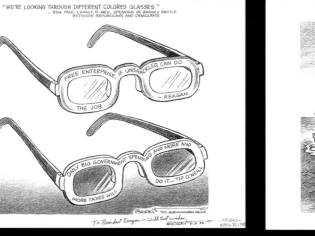

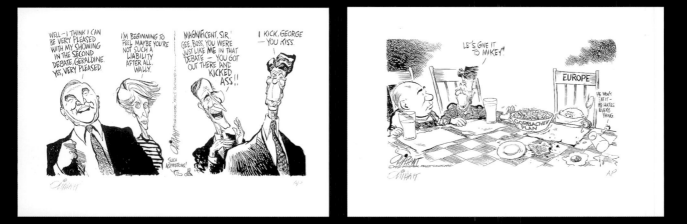

"It's my job to solve all the country's problems, and it's your job to make sure no one finds out about it." —Ronald Reagan, to reporters at the White House Correspondents' Association Dinner, 1985

The president toasts Australian prime minister Malcolm Fraser at a 1981 White House state dinner.

HIS VALUES "Absolutely the first thing he did every night when he came upstairs to the residence was talk to Nancy. He enjoyed just being with her." —Sheila Tate, press secretary to the first lady

LIFE AT THE WHITE HOUSE

Admirers marveled (and critics carped) at how President Reagan was able to maintain a nine-to-five workday while holding the world's most complex job. In part, he could do it because he kept to a schedule that seldom varied.

The Reagans awoke each morning to a 7:30 call from a White House operator. Soon thereafter, a butler appeared with a light breakfast and the morning newspapers. A little before nine, dressed in his customary suit and tie, Reagan kissed his wife good-bye and took the elevator from the family quarters on the second floor of the White House to the ground floor, where a Secret Service agent escorted him past the Rose Garden to the Oval Office in the West Wing.

A staff meeting with Reagan's top aides and Vice President George Bush began the official day at 9:00. At 9:30, the president's national security adviser briefed the group on international affairs. Unless the president had a speaking engagement outside the White House, his day was a succession of meetings—with cabinet members, his staff, foreign dignitaries, and members of congress. Around 5:00 P.M., Reagan returned to the East Wing for a half-hour workout. Then, if there were no state dinner or other function that required their presence, he and Nancy dined alone on trays in the president's study while watching the evening news. "So much of your life is on display that to be alone and relaxed," said Mrs. Reagan, "is a luxury we looked forward to."

Both Reagans wrote in their respective journals before turning in each night. Then after some light reading, they'd fall asleep around ten or eleven.

During many of their days in the White House, Nancy Reagan's schedule was only slightly less hectic than her husband's, filled with meetings and phone calls and public appearances, replete with the unofficial but vital duties unique to first ladies. She gave countless dinners and luncheons, once a month hosting state dinners with her husband. Much time, however, was devoted to her two favorite projects: Foster Grandparents, which benefited both the elderly and the youngsters they mentored, and Just Say No, the program she herself conceived to help the nation's youth avoid drugs. Under her leadership, hundreds of thousands of children made commitments to remain drug-free—and thousands more would continue to do so long after the Reagans left the White House.

The first lady oversees the decorating of the White House Christmas tree in December 1982.

"First ladies, I discovered, are one of the taxpayers' biggest bargains; they're unpaid, work full schedules, and are always on the move. From combating drugs to restoring the beauty of the White House to helping me represent our country overseas, Nancy was among the hardest-working of all our first ladies." —Ronald Reagan

The president offers a toast (above, left) during a private White House dinner for the prince and princess of Japan in October 1987. British prime minister Margaret Thatcher and her husband, Denis, far left, visited the Reagans on several occasions, and the first couple entertained Queen Elizabeth and Prince Philip, left, during the monarch's visit to Washington in March 1983.

"In eight years, I hosted close to a hundred Christmas parties—not to mention *dozens of official* dinners, lunches, meetings with wives of foreign dignitaries, receptions, arrival ceremonies, awards, speaking engagements, political dinners, fund-raisers, and dozens of trips. I was very involved in planning White House events, right down to the details. I loved doing it." —Nancy Reagan

Famous visitors to the Reagan White House included Britain's Princess Diana and American queen of comedy Lucille Ball. At right is the personal china tea set that Mrs. Reagan used to entertain. Its design features the Reagans' intials, individually and in combination.

"As soon as he entered the room, you could almost feel the aura about him. He could transform a rather stiff group into enthusiasts with that great smile and engaging manner of his."

"One of the great things about being president is that you can invite anyone you want to lunch or dinner, and chances are they'll come." —Ronald Reagan

Sipping tea in the Yellow Oval Room, the president and first lady entertain King Carl XVI and Queen Silvia of Sweden in a 1988 visit to Washington.

The president and first lady embrace a young girl representing the March of Dimes after a 1981 ceremony honoring the organization in the East Room of the White House.

"I was always impressed with the president's sensitivity to everyone who was in a meeting with him. If he saw anyone there who seemed anxious to say something, he figured it must be important, so [he] drew it out." —David Laux, director of Asian Affairs, National Security Council

THE PERFECT GENTLEMAN

After Ronald Reagan was shot, Vice President George Bush visited him in the hospital and found the president of the United States on his knees in the bathroom, mopping spilled water off the floor. Bush protested that a nurse should be doing that. No, Reagan said. Against doctors' orders, he had gotten out of bed and given himself a sponge bath. If the nurse was found cleaning up the mess, she might get into trouble.

It was that kindness—a consideration that encompassed people of all strata—that made Reagan so loved by those who worked closest with him, and by millions of Americans who never even met him. "He was probably the sweetest, most innocent man ever to serve in the Oval Office," wrote author and former Reagan speechwriter Peggy Noonan.

The president set aside time each day to read at least fifty of the thousands of letters that poured into the White House. And he answered at least ten a day. If the letters told of problems, he took them seriously, and personally. One young man wrote of not having a suit to get married in. Reagan sent him one of his own. A soldier from California asked him to send his wife flowers for their anniversary. Reagan deliv-

Visiting the National Institute of Health in Bethesda, Maryland, President Reagan takes a moment to visit with a young patient.

ered them in person. Often he sent money. When a bank refused to cash a hundred-dollar check, contending the presidential signature was worth more than the amount, Reagan had an aide call the bank and make sure the recipient got the cash. When an elderly woman wrote of troubles with Social Security, he made sure the problem was straightened out. He also invited her to the White House for coffee.

"He never thought he was stooping to these people," wrote Noonan, "he didn't think he was better, and he was possessed of an intuitive sense of the purpose of royalty." That is to say, the king is the people's servant.

Reagan understood this, never overlooking or taking for granted any kindness—seemingly immune from the arrogance and thoughtlessness that so often go with power. When Connecticut schoolchildren sent him some inexpensive stationery they had decorated for him, he used it for years. When he wrote a letter for his secretary to type, he neatly printed the address at the top so she would not have to look it up. It was a small gesture but typical of his courtesy, a courtliness that was inborn and old school. He was, as former first lady Barbara Bush summed up, "always a gentleman."

HIS VALUES "It seemed for a time as if there were back-to-back hijackings and hostage-takings. He would focus on these problems intensely, but if we then had someone coming in to be honored, he would put the crisis aside for the moment, smile, and treat the visitor as if he or she were the most important person in the world."—Kathy Osborne, secretary and longtime assistant to Ronald Reagan

The president and first lady enjoy a TV dinner, above, with Rudolf Hines, Reagan's pen pal, in September 1984. The year before, the White House had adopted Congress Heights Elementary School of Washington, D.C., in an effort to begin a mentoring program among the White House staff and underprivileged children. Staffers would attend school events, speak, and answer questions. Most did not participate in the pen pal program, but Reagan was eager to do so and chose to correspond with Hines. The two kept in touch via letters throughout Reagan's presidency.

"He called me at home after my mother died in 1983. Her death seemed merciful, for she had been ill a long time, but I was surprised how little I had been prepared for it. When I said as much to Reagan, he responded, 'You are never prepared for the death of your mother,' then proceeded to tell me his feelings when his own mother had died under similar circumstances. I was consoled and overcome." —Lou Cannon, journalist and Reagan biographer

"Ronald Reagan was such a joy to be around. My ten years working for him in various capacities were crowded with so many incidents of his kindness and thoughtfulness that it's hard to remember them all."

—Nancy Clark Reynolds, former aide

President Reagan chats with school-children in the Oval Office for the taping of a children's television show in early 1988.

"He always conducted himself with a great amount of courtesy. I never saw him be rude to anyone, though some were rude to him. I never saw him react in anger at a high-level meeting, nor did he throw his weight around. He always spoke softly.... He knew how the American people wanted a president to conduct himself, and that is exactly what he did."

Reagan gets a rousing reception at the 1984 Republican National Convention in Dallas. He had been unopposed in the primaries, and the outcome of the general election was never seriously in doubt.

HIS VISION "I regarded the 1984 presidential election as pivotal— not because I wanted to live in the White House for four more years, but because I believed the gains we'd made during the previous four years were in jeopardy." —Ronald Reagan

FOUR MORE IN '84

After his first three years in office, President Reagan's reelection in 1984 seemed a near certainty: America's economic recovery had begun, people were feeling proud and optimistic again, and his personal popularity was soaring. He was eager to run, concerned that his Democratic opponent, former vice president Walter Mondale, would reverse the recovery with big tax hikes. Besides, Reagan felt there was still much more to accomplish. He wanted to balance the budget, simplify the tax code, and pursue the foreign policy that, he believed, would eventually cripple the Soviet empire and reduce the threat of nuclear war.

Nancy Reagan was less enthusiastic about another four years. "Had it been up to me, Ronald Reagan might well have been a one-term president," she said. "I yearned for more family time and more privacy. I missed my friends and my family, and I missed California." She also feared for her husband's safety. But she put her misgivings aside, and on January 29, 1984, the president announced he would seek reelection.

Given his early lead, the race was clearly his to lose—and at one point he almost managed it. Two televised debates were scheduled, the first on October 7 in Louisville, Kentucky. Overprepared, crammed by aides with facts and statistics that curbed his flexibility and cramped his natural style, he stumbled badly. Pundits began asking whether, at seventy-three, he was too old for another term. In its post-debate headline, even the *Wall Street Journal*, which usually supported him, asked: "IS OLDEST U.S. PRESIDENT NOW SHOWING HIS AGE? REAGAN DEBATE PERFORMANCE INVITES OPEN SPECULATION ON HIS ABILITY TO SERVE."

Two weeks later, however, Reagan went into the second debate in Kansas City determined to be himself. Age was on everyone's mind, and one reporter was quick to ask about it. It was then that Reagan came up with one of his inspired one-liners. "I am not going to exploit for political purposes," he said, "my opponent's youth and inexperience."

Even Mondale laughed, and Americans—watching the moment replayed on television again and again—concluded that the president was still very much in control. In November, he won by a landslide, carrying every state but Mondale's native Minnesota.

The Republican ticket looks justifiably confident on the August 8, 1984, cover of *Time*.

"Ronnie was determined to run again. There were still things he wanted to do. He also thought it had been too long since an American president had served two full terms in office. In the end, it was just a matter of convincing me. Looking back, I'm glad I lost that argument." —Nancy Reagan

By 1984, Americans had caught Reagan's confidence. It was, as the president's reelection campaign optimistically reminded voters, "morning again in America."

HIS VOICE "The American people liked Ronald Reagan and reelected him in one of the biggest landslides in history because he trusted them and he conveyed to them that they need not be bound, tied down by class, or race, or childhood misfortune, or poverty, or bureaucracy. They, the people, could make something of themselves; indeed, they could remake themselves, endlessly."

—George Shultz, secretary of state

A Voice for the World

"We meant to change a nation,

If "stay the course" had been the byword for Ronald Reagan's first term as president, "peace through strength" was the motto for the second. The mid- and late-1980s saw his greatest triumphs in international affairs—the full flowering of the Reagan doctrine.

The Truman doctrine had sought to contain communism; the Reagan doctrine meant to diminish it—and, just possibly, to destroy the Soviet Union itself, to cause it to topple under the weight of its own flawed system. This was always the end in view as Reagan negotiated with a new Soviet leader, Mikhail Gorbachev. Reagan assessed that Gorbachev was a new sort of Soviet, a man it might be possible to deal with. He was right. At their first summit, in Geneva, the two developed a liking for each other. Yet despite the burgeoning friendship, Gorbachev learned early in their private talks that this American president was seeking neither appeasement nor accommodation, that he would not pursue peace at any price: Reagan made it clear that if the Cold War had to continue, the United States intended to win it.

When the two met again, in Reykjavik, Gorbachev tested Reagan's resolve with a tempting offer—the possibility of a nuclear-free world if Reagan would only abandon America's Strategic Defense Initiative. But once again Reagan stood firm. Refusing the bait, the president forced Gorbachev into a fateful choice: Try

and instead we changed a world."

to match American technology and economic might or forsake Soviet dreams of expansion and world domination. Reagan's unshakable determination turned out to be a lever that moved the world.

In 1987, at the Berlin Wall, Reagan issued another forceful challenge to the Soviets, calling on Mikhail Gorbachev to inaugurate a new era of freedom for Europe. The very sight of the graffiti-smeared monolith of concrete and barbed wire that for years had divided East from West, totalitarian bloc from free world, angered the president. It was, he said, "as stark a symbol as anyone could ever expect to see of the contrast between two different political systems: on one side, people held captive by a failed and corrupt totalitarian government, on the other, freedom, enterprise, prosperity." Standing before the wall, Reagan dared the Soviets to give substance to their promises of greater freedom and prosperity for Iron Curtain countries. "Mr. Gorbachev," the president demanded, "tear down this wall!" Within three years, the decades-old symbol of tyranny would indeed crumble.

But along with the triumphs of the second term, there were also troughs—deep ones. Toward the end of 1986, the Reagan presidency faced its gravest threat: the Iran-Contra scandal. It was a complex affair involving the sale of arms to Iran, the effort to free American hostages held by terrorists in Lebanon, and the illegal flow of money from the arms sale to U.S.-backed guerrillas in Nicaragua. The president was accused of trading arms for hostages and suspected of sanctioning the allocation of money to the Contra rebels. He explained that he had not, as he saw it, negotiated with terrorists, and he insisted he had been unaware that members of his National Security Council had been illegally funding the Contras.

Even so, his popularity plummeted. Many Americans obviously doubted his word, a fact that surprised and saddened him. "For the first time in my life," he wrote later, "people didn't believe me. I had told the truth, but they still didn't believe me." Frustrated at having his integrity questioned, he nevertheless pressed on through a storm of criticism to continue with his own agenda, confident that he had done nothing wrong.

In the end, various investigations exonerated him: He had shown poor judgment, perhaps, in the arms sale, but he had neither lied about his knowledge of funding for the Contras nor tried to cover up the facts. He salvaged his presidency and, more important to him, his bond of trust with the American people. By the end of his second term, he would have the highest approval rating of any president since Franklin Delano Roosevelt.

HIS VISION "Freedom is the right to question and change the established way of doing things. It is the continuing revolution of the marketplace. It is the understanding that allows us to recognize shortcomings and seek solutions. It is the right to put forth an idea, scoffed at by the experts,

and watch it catch fire among the people. It is the right to dream—to follow your dream or stick to your conscience, even if you're the only one in a sea of doubters." —Ronald Reagan, address to students at Moscow State University, May 31, 1988

President Reagan and Pope John Paul II meet briefly in Fairbanks, Alaska, in 1984. Both were in transit, the president on his way home from a trip to China, the pope on his way to South Korea.

Moments after lifting off from Cape Canaveral, the space shuttle *Challenger* explodes, killing all aboard. The president said that the day of the disaster was "one of the hardest days I ever had to spend in the Oval Office."

"This America ... was built on heroism and noble sacrifice. It was built by men and women like our seven star voyagers, who answered a call beyond duty, who gave more than was expected or required, and who gave it little thought to worldly reward."

—Ronald Reagan, remarks at the memorial service for the crew of the space shuttle *Challenger* in Houston, Texas

DISASTER IN SPACE

By 1986, many Americans were almost blasé about space shuttle expeditions—a testament to the phenomenal success of the United States' space program. But the launch of the space shuttle *Challenger* on January 28 was anticipated with unusual interest: This mission would be the first to carry into space a civilian, a young mother and schoolteacher named Christa McAuliffe.

Thus millions of Americans were watching on television as the mission began. They saw McAuliffe and her six fellow crew members, clad in their space suits, smile and wave as they walked toward the shuttle. They watched as, shortly before noon, the great missile lifted off the launch pad at Cape Canaveral. And they watched seconds later as something went terribly wrong: A huge bloom of white smoke appeared against the crystalline blue of the Florida sky. The *Challenger* had exploded, killing all aboard.

Across the nation, pride and excitement turned to shock and horror. Nowhere, save in the homes of the victims, was the pain more acute than in the White House. President Reagan was scheduled to give his State of the Union address to Congress that night. He postponed the

Stricken, the president watches a televised rerun of the *Challenger* catastrophe.

speech and delivered instead a brief, televised address about the *Challenger* disaster. It was widely regarded as one of his finest speeches, one that soothed grief even while it promised that the exploration of space would go on.

To the families of the seven, he said, "Your loved ones were daring and brave, and they had that special grace, that special spirit that says, 'Give me a challenge, and I'll meet it with joy.' They had a hunger to explore the universe and discover its truths."

Then the president spoke to the nation's schoolchildren who had watched the disaster on television. "I know it is hard to understand," he said, "but sometimes painful things like this happen. It's all part of the process of exploration and discovery. It's all part of taking a chance and expanding man's horizons. The future doesn't belong to the fainthearted; it belongs to the brave. The *Challenger* crew was pulling us into the future, and we'll continue to follow them."

He ended his speech with quotes from the poem "High Flight": "We will never forget them, nor the last time we saw them, this morning, as they prepared for their journey and waved goodbye and 'slipped the surly bonds of earth' to 'touch the face of God.'"

HIS VOICE "As a leader, his ability to communicate was especially important in times of adversity. When the space shuttle *Challenger* was lost . . . his immediate response was to try to calm people and have them reflect on the bigger picture; his aim was not to eliminate grief, but to direct it toward the ultimate healing process." —Edwin Meese, U.S. attorney general and chief of staff to the governor

Reagan, Gorbachev, and their aides convene in Geneva for the first U.S.-USSR summit. The president went to Geneva with his favorite Russian proverb in mind: *Dovorey no provorey*. "Trust, but verify."

"We don't mistrust each other because we're armed. We're armed because we mistrust each other." —Ronald Reagan to Soviet leader Mikhail Gorbachev

BREAKING THE ICE

Asked in his first term why he had not met with a Soviet leader, President Reagan remarked, "They keep dying on me." It was true. Leonid Brezhnev, Yuri Andropov, and Konstantin Chernenko all died in rapid succession in the early 1980s. Then a new man appeared at the USSR's helm, one who—although he had no such intention—would preside over the dissolution of the Soviet empire.

Mikhail Gorbachev was youngish, amiable, cosmopolitan, and media-friendly—utterly unlike any of his predecessors. He introduced his nation to *glasnost* ("openness") and *perestroika* ("restructuring") and was hailed in the West as a political genius. Reagan correctly gauged that his Soviet counterpart was, at heart, a true-believing Marxist who vainly hoped to rescue the Soviets' foundering socialism by reforming it. Still, he was impressed that his closest ally, Margaret Thatcher, had liked Gorbachev. "We can do business together," she had said.

Reagan and Gorbachev first met at a summit meeting in a lakeside chateau in Geneva, Switzerland, in November 1985. On the first afternoon, Reagan suggested that the two, with their translators, chat privately in a boathouse on the

A mock movie poster drawing its title inspiration from the Reagan movie *Bedtime for Bonzo* shows the president taking a hard line with one of Gorbachev's predecessors, Leonid Brezhnev.

chateau's grounds. In front of a pleasant fire, they made small talk. Then came a crucial moment, as Reagan would later relate. "I do hope for the sake of our children that we can find some way to avert this terrible, escalating arms race . . ." began Reagan. Gorbachev smiled, perhaps concluding that despite his "evil empire" rhetoric, Reagan was eager to maintain the status quo. Then Reagan finished his thought: "Because if we can't, America will not lose it, I assure you."

If Gorbachev found Reagan tougher than expected, Reagan sized up Gorbachev as an ideologue and a hard negotiator, but also as a man of conscience. He liked his forward-thinking Russian adversary, hailing him as "a new kind of Soviet leader." At the summit's close, the two men shook hands and signed an agreement to reduce their nuclear stockpiles.

The next summit, the following October in Reykjavik, Iceland, at first promised even greater things. Gorbachev offered to eliminate all of the Soviets' medium-range missiles in Europe and cut their strategic arsenal almost in half. He even agreed in principle to a plan for both nations to eliminate their nuclear weapons altogether. It seemed too good to be

HIS VOICE "He believed what he said in that simple, unforgettable line declaring unequivocally that America would not lose the arms race. Ronald Reagan believed it, and so did Mikhail Gorbachev. And, as they say, the rest is history. Ronald Reagan thinks it may have been his best scene. I'm convinced of it." —Pete Wilson, governor of California

true—and it was. Toward the end of the talks, Gorbachev demanded one concession: America must abandon its Strategic Defense Initiative or the deal would be off.

Reagan's advisers begged him to accept: Why throw away the possibility of a nuclear-free world for a pie-in-the-sky research project that might never be a reality? But Reagan felt he was being blackmailed, and he was furious at Gorbachev, who refused to budge even when Reagan promised that America would share its SDI research with any nation that wanted it, assuring an end to the nuclear threat. He also knew that if the Soviets attached such importance to SDI, it meant they believed—as he did—that the Americans could pull it off. And an effective defense against Soviet missiles would mean a new phase in the arms race, one the economically tottering USSR could not hope to win.

Tension is etched on the faces of participants during the second summit, in Reykjavik. Reagan and Secretary of State George Shultz (standing) had been euphoric over the talks' progress until Gorbachev, at the last minute, dashed their hopes.

"The meeting is over," Reagan told a stunned Gorbachev. "We're leaving." As the Americans made their way to their limousines the next morning, Gorbachev approached the president apologetically. "I don't know what else I could have done," he said. Reagan eyed him coldly. "You could have said yes."

Reagan returned home to a predictable barrage of criticism from the pundits—but not from the people. Polls showed that three out of four Americans supported his hard-line position. He followed up on the summit by persuading West Germany to station cruise missiles along its eastern border, virtually neutralizing the Soviet nuclear threat to Western Europe. Gorbachev faced a choice: He could try to match the United States in a renewed arms race, or he could use his resources to attempt to shore up the wrecked Soviet economy. In December 1987, having jettisoned his "nonnegotiable" demand that America give up SDI, he arrived in Washington to sign the intermediate-range nuclear forces (INF) treaty. Apparently, he had made up his mind.

The INF treaty was historic. For the first time, the two superpowers agreed to eliminate an entire class of nuclear weapons. But the effects were more far-reaching than that: Though few realized it at the time, it was a signal of surrender. Reagan's stand at Reykjavik, many historians would come to believe, marked the beginning of the end of the Soviet Union, and with it the Cold War.

"He had tremendous stamina. He had a compass that worked from beginning to end. I detected in Gorbachev a panicky sense, and at various times, among some of our own delegation. But the president was just steady, steady, steady, from beginning to end.... When the hooker was revealed, he was balanced. His judgment was solid." —Richard Perle, assistant secretary of defense

HIS VISION "President Reagan's refusal to trade away SDI for the apparent near fulfilment of his dream of a nuclear-free world was crucial to the victory over communism. He called the Soviets' bluff. The Russians may have scored an immediate propaganda victory when the talks broke down. But they had lost the game." —Margaret Thatcher, prime minister of Great Britain

Reagan and Gorbachev confront each other in Iceland, with the amity that had characterized their Geneva meeting nowhere in sight. When the president left Reykjavik he was disappointed and furious, believing that Gorbachev had "brought me to Iceland with one purpose: to kill the Strategic Defense Initiative."

Gorbachev travels to Washington, above, to sign the historic INF treaty. Two years earlier, getting to know each other in Geneva, right, Reagan and Gorbachev stand before the fireplace in the Fleur D'Eau Pool House where they met privately early in the 1985 summit.

HIS VISION "At the time, the Soviet Union, with its huge armies and its awesome nuclear arsenal, still posed quite a threat. Reagan's greatest insight might have been his grasp of the great vulnerability behind the menacing facade." —Seweryn Bialer and Joan Afferica of *Foreign Affairs* magazine

"In a 1988 visit to the USSR, Gorbachev told me: 'I am familiar with your Constitution, but I wish your husband could stay on for another four years.' It was fascinating to hear. While it's possible he was being polite, I believe he was sincere. He and Ronnie had developed a mutual respect and affection." —Nancy Reagan

"Reagan was exactly correct in knowing that the resources of the U.S. could not be matched by those of the enemy.... Reagan belongs on Mount Rushmore, and he'll be there, after the carpers die off."

—William F. Buckley, Jr., founder of *National Review* and author

Mikhail Gorbachev and Ronald Reagan, above, sign the treaty eliminating all intermediate-range nuclear missiles. At left, they toast the occasion.

NEGOTIATIONS WITH GORBACHEV

"Reagan pushed me one step more and then one step more till we got to the precipice, and then he wanted one step more." —Mikhail Gorbachev, general secretary of the USSR

Reagan breaks into a nervous smile moments before meeting General Secretary Mikhail Gorbachev in Geneva, Switzerland.

Reagan, Gorbachev, and Raisa Gorbachev shelter under umbrellas (above top) during a White House departure ceremony honoring the Soviet leader. Later, the two leaders acknowledge cheers from Washington well-wishers while walking on the south grounds of the White House.

HIS VALUES "Reagan wasn't a 'hidden hand' president who played his cards under the table. His true genius was that he put all his cards on the table and still managed to win most of the time." —Kenneth Adelman, arms control adviser

ACHTUNG!
SIE VERLASSEN
JETZT
WEST BERLIN

President Reagan speaks at the Brandenburg Gate. The sign on the Berlin Wall behind him reads: "Attention! You are now leaving West Berlin," but very few Germans ever voluntarily made the passage from West to the Communist East.

HIS VISION "For most of us who fought in the twilight struggle against communism, the prospect of victory seemed a long distance off. But Ronald Reagan didn't see it that way. He didn't believe in walls. That was his genius." —John McCain, senator from Arizona

AT THE WALL

On August 13, 1961, the sun rose on a stretch of new barbed wire that snaked through Berlin, marking the twenty-eight-mile route where a wall would soon stand, dividing East Berlin from West, communist world from free. Since the Allies had divided Germany after World War II, some 2.5 million people had fled from East to West. East Germany was building the wall to stop them. Almost eight hundred people would die trying to cross it in the nearly three decades it would stand, the most detested symbol of communist repression in the world.

On June 12, 1987, President Reagan stood at Brandenburg Gate—a closed gate— once a symbol of German grandeur, now a part of the hated wall. Tens of thousands of West Berliners had gathered to hear him speak. On the other side, East Berliners listened, too, despite police efforts to hold them back.

"To those listening in East Berlin," Reagan said, "I address my remarks to you just as surely as to those standing here before me. For I join you, as I join your fellow countrymen in the West, in this firm, this unalterable belief: *Es gibt nur ein Berlin.* [There is only one Berlin.] Behind me stands a wall that encircles the free sectors of this city, part of a vast system of barriers that divides the entire continent of Europe. From the Baltic, south, those barriers cut across Germany in a gash of barbed wire, concrete, dog runs, and guard towers. Farther south, there may be no visible, no obvious wall. But there remain armed guards and checkpoints all the same."

Standing at the gate, he said, "every man is a Berliner, forced to look upon a scar." Then the president challenged Mikhail Gorbachev to make good on his promises of reform. "There is one sign the Soviets can make that would be unmistakable," Reagan said, "that would advance dramatically the cause of freedom and peace. General Secretary Gorbachev, if you seek peace, if you seek prosperity for the Soviet Union and Eastern Europe, if you seek liberalization: Come here to this gate! Mr. Gorbachev, open this gate! Mr. Gorbachev, tear down this wall!"

At midnight on November 9, 1989, the gates did open, and thousands of Germans streamed toward the West. Berliners began attacking the wall with picks and chisels. Construction crews would follow. Within months it would vanish, crumbling along with the regime that had erected it.

GLOBAL DEMOCRACY

★

Reagan's vision of freedom was far-reaching: All people, he believed, should have the right to govern themselves. A lifelong champion of global democracy, President Reagan continually denounced communism and other forms of tyranny even when others thought the fight was futile. Just days before he challenged Mikhail Gorbachev at the Berlin Wall, Reagan encouraged Europeans with these seemingly prophetic words: "If I can leave the young people of Europe with one message it is this: History is on the side of the free."

"Ronald Reagan meant what he said, and he was right. His speech is permanent testimony to his belief in the power of freedom.... This was no rash prophecy but the firm conviction of an American president who saw in Berlin the qualities that made his own country great: creativity, willpower, courage, and the love of freedom." —Helmut Kohl, chancellor of the Federal Republic of Germany

IRAN-CONTRA

On November 3, 1986, a Beirut magazine ran a story alleging that the United States was selling arms to Iran in return for Iranian efforts to obtain the release of American hostages held by Muslim terrorists in Lebanon. Picked up by the American press, the story ignited a firestorm. It seemed that Ronald Reagan, who had vowed never to negotiate with terrorists, was trading arms for hostages. Worse, he was dealing with one of America's most bitter enemies, Iran's aging theocrat Ayatollah Khomeini.

Later in November, the second half of what came to be known as the Iran-Contra scandal broke: Members of Reagan's administration had illegally funneled some of the proceeds from the arms sale to the Contras, guerrilla fighters opposing the communist Sandinista regime in Nicaragua.

The president immediately went to the American people with his side. He had not traded arms for hostages, he maintained, nor had he dealt with Khomeini. What he had approved was a complex deal involving the state of Israel and certain moderate Iranian leaders who hoped to form the nucleus of a new and more friendly Iranian government after the ayatollah's death. Israel sold arms to the moderates,

On November 25, 1986, the president briefs members of Congress on the National Security Council's involvement in the Iran-Contra situation.

and America replaced the arms to Israel. Part of the deal did involve the moderates intervening with the Beirut terrorists to get the hostages released, and some had been freed.

Reagan assured Americans he had neither known of nor sanctioned money to the Contras. That had been done by a member of the National Security Council staff, marine colonel Oliver North, and North's boss, NSC chief John Poindexter, had known about it. As soon the president discovered this, Poindexter resigned and North was fired. Reagan ordered his administration to comply fully with congressional investigations and even appointed a special prosecutor to look into the matter.

Despite Reagan's full disclosure, Iran-Contra cast a pall on his presidency. His approval rating dropped from nearly 70 percent to around 35 percent, his critics talked of impeachment, and even some of his supporters didn't stand with him. But the people's trust began returning after various investigations revealed that Reagan had told the truth. The arms deal had been a mistake, perhaps, but an honest one, and Reagan had known nothing about money being channeled to the Contras. His presidency may have been damaged, but it rebounded strongly.

"I take full responsibility for my own actions and for those of my administration. As angry as I may be about activities undertaken without my knowledge, I am still accountable for those activities. As disappointed as I may be in some who served me, I'm still the one who must answer to the

American people for this behavior. And as personally distasteful as I find secret bank accounts and diverted funds—well, as the navy would say, this happened on my watch." —Ronald Reagan, address to the nation on the Tower Commission report, March 4, 1987

Reagan fields questions about Iran-Contra at a mid-November news conference. He wanted to help the Nicaraguan rebels, but insisted he never authorized his staff to overstep legal bounds to achieve that end.

Ronald Reagan welcomes an old friend to Camp David in the fall of 1986. Though she came on working visits, Margaret Thatcher was one of the few heads of state invited by the Reagans to their private retreat.

"Throughout the eight years of my presidency, no alliance we had was stronger than the one between the United States and the United Kingdom." —Ronald Reagan

THE GREAT COMMUNICATOR AND THE IRON LADY

Ronald Reagan fondly referred to Britain's Margaret Thatcher as "the other woman in my life," and not entirely in jest. His tenure as president coincided with hers as the United Kingdom's prime minister, and over the years they shared a unique personal and political bond.

When they first met in April 1975, he was considering a run for the presidency in 1976. She had recently been elected the first woman to head Britain's Conservative Party. They were introduced in England by a mutual friend. "I liked her immediately," Reagan would recall. "She was warm, feminine, gracious, and intelligent—and it was evident from our first words that we were soul mates when it came to reducing government and expanding economic freedom."

They were on the same side on most issues. Reagan particularly admired Mrs. Thatcher's success in reviving Great Britain's faltering economy by downsizing government and returning enterprises to the private sector. And Thatcher was the most loyal backer abroad of Reagan's tough foreign policy stands. In 1986, for instance, when the president ordered bombing strikes on Libya in retaliation for the Libyan-backed terrorist bombing of a Berlin disco, allies France and Italy refused to let American planes cross their airspace; but Thatcher lent Reagan her full support. Most of all, she applauded his firm stand against the Soviets, particularly his refusal to trade away SDI at Reykjavik.

Of course, the two did not always agree. When Reagan ordered the Grenada rescue mission, Mrs. Thatcher protested that the island was part of the British Commonwealth, and the United States had no business there. But even when they differed, she admired his toughness, and he hers. Once, when she was berating him long-distance over some disagreement, Reagan held out the phone so his aides could hear and said with a smile, "Isn't she *marvelous?*"

The other woman in the president's life also got along well with the primary one, his wife. The Reagans, extremely protective of their privacy at Camp David, nevertheless invited Mrs. Thatcher there twice. They held their first state dinner in her honor. And in the White House family quarters, Nancy Reagan hung a poster that amused her no end: A picture substituting her husband for Clark Gable and Margaret Thatcher for Vivian Leigh in a passionate scene from *Gone with the Wind.*

Reagan and Thatcher exchange views at the 1985 economic summit in Bonn. When it came to economic theory, they were of one mind.

"Even though she was a close friend of the president, she almost invariably called him Mr. President, rather than Ron or anything like that. She had great affection and huge admiration for him.... He was a tremendous friend and ally." —Sir Charles Powell, deputy head of mission and private secretary to Margaret Thatcher

RETREAT FROM THE WORLD

It is ironic that Ronald Reagan the movie star was never typecast as a cowboy, for riding a horse over a rugged landscape was among the things he loved best in the world. He had learned to enjoy riding during his youthful days as a sportscaster, and as president he still preferred a saddle to any other seat. Riding afforded him escape from the pressures of office, a chance to reflect and gain perspective. So when time allowed, he and Nancy headed for one of the two places that offered horses, open space, solitude, and a chance to relax: Camp David near Washington and their beloved Rancho del Cielo in California.

Camp David is the presidential retreat in Maryland's Catoctin Mountain, seventy miles north of Washington, only a few minutes by helicopter. It features stately trees, an expanse of rolling land, and a scattering of rustic cabins for the president and his family and guests. The presidential cabin, Aspen Lodge, is snug and homey, with a large room for living and dining, a bedroom suite, guest room, study, and kitchen. A picture window in the living room frames the beautiful panorama of a tree-fringed valley.

It was a much-needed retreat for the Reagans. "As much as Ronnie and I loved the White House," said Nancy Reagan, "we found it very difficult to live in a place where you couldn't ever go out for a walk. We're both outdoor types, and it didn't take long before we started feeling cooped up. Thank God for Camp David! I never expected that we would use it practically every weekend, but it became a regular and welcome part of our routine."

Less accessible than the presidential compound but even more cherished was the Reagans' private getaway, Rancho del Cielo, or Ranch in the Sky, in the Santa Ynez mountains north of Santa Barbara, only a few miles from the Pacific Ocean. "Ronnie is so happy there!" Mrs. Reagan said. "He loves to be outside, building fences, cutting down trees and brush, and chopping wood for the two fireplaces, which are our only source of heat. The ranch is on top of a mountain, and when you get up there, the rest of the world disappears."

The Reagans bought the 688-acre ranch after leaving Sacramento and added a room to its tiny adobe house, which, though modest, remained their favorite home. The land's majestic scenery and network of riding trails captivated them both.

"From the first day we saw it, Rancho del Cielo cast a spell over us," Reagan said. "No place before or since has ever given Nancy and me the joy and serenity it does."

Reagan used this English saddle when riding at Rancho del Cielo. Now it is displayed in the Ronald Reagan Presidential Library.

"The White House has magnificent quarters and we were very well treated there, but you are kind of a bird in a gilded cage, and they don't open the door very often to let the bird out. Camp David—and the ranch, when we were able to get there—became our haven." —Nancy Reagan

"It was a place where he could renew himself and rejuvenate himself. He would disappear into the hills for hours with the chain saw or just on horseback, he was happy as a clam doing his ranch thing."

—Ron Reagan, son, describing Rancho del Cielo

The first couple explores one of the half dozen riding trails at the ranch in this photo by Harry Benson. "Rancho del Cielo could make you feel as if you are on a cloud looking down at the world," Reagan said.

A photo from Mrs. Reagan's private collection shows the president putting in a day's work at the ranch. He enjoyed the physical labor. Below is a pair of his work gloves.

The president helps his lady dismount after a ride at Rancho del Cielo in 1983. At left, they exchange a kiss over breakfast. The ranch house had only about 1,500 square feet of living space, but its intimate charm enchanted them both.

"One night [on assignment at Reagan's ranch], I was talking live with Barbara Walters on 20/20 and she asked me what was going on. I said, 'Nothing much. We have the ranch report and, once again, he chopped wood and cleared brush. I suspect that just before he gets there, they haul up truckloads of brush and wood for him to chop because, if he chopped as much as they say he does, there wouldn't be any trees left on the ranch.' Well,

JUST A LOOK BACK TO THE MALIBU RANCH WHILE GOU.

Photos of life on the ranch are kept in a leather-bound family album, with captions penned in the president's own hand. The album chronic.es renovations the Reagans made to Rancho del Cielo over the years. There are also pictures of friends and family members, human and otherwise: One of their dogs, Victory, is shown at right. At left is a pair of Reagan's riding boots.

Reagan was watching, and the next day, I'm told, he called his ranch foreman and said he wanted all the brush he had cleared over the last week or ten days piled up in one place by the house. They did, and he had a photographer take pictures of it from all angles. He sent me one of the photos, on which he had written, 'Dear Sam, Here's the proof I chopped it all with my own little hatchet.' Talk about focus!" Sam Donaldson, White House correspondent, ABC News

"The president's home at Camp David, called Aspen, is a beautiful rustic house with beamed ceilings, wood-paneled walls, and big windows that look out at the forest. Just as we did at Rancho del Cielo, Nancy and I experienced a sense of liberation at Camp David that we

never found in Washington. Because the perimeter was guarded, we could just open a door and take a walk. That's a freedom, incidentally, that you don't fully appreciate until you've lost it." —Ronald Reagan

In a January snowfall or the spectacular foliage of autumn, Camp David afforded the Reagans beauty, privacy, and quiet time away from the pressures of Washington. The president called the retreat "a slice of heaven."

CAMP DAVID

HIS VALUES *"I had a tremendous feeling of release when we got to Camp David. It was so important to us, in keeping our perspective on things, to be able to be there alone, to have quiet time together to think and reflect and get our thoughts in order."* —Nancy Reagan

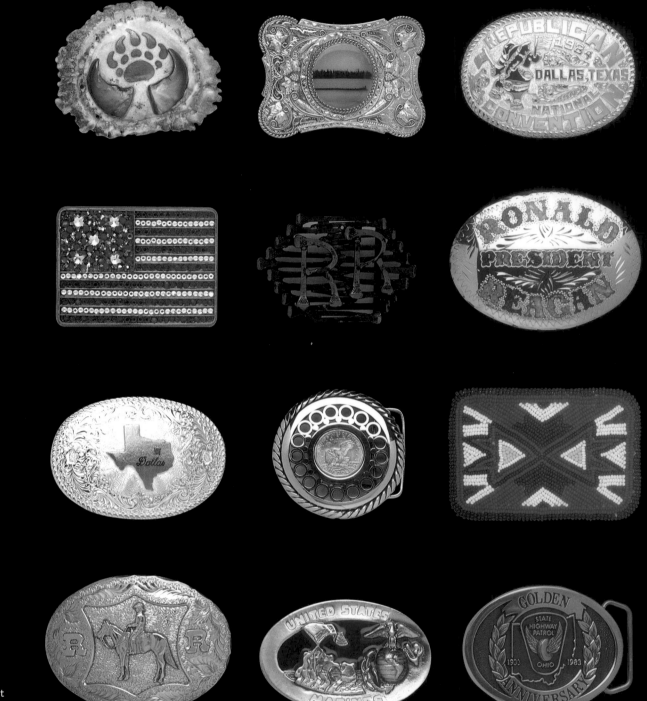

Reagan collected belt buckles, and he particularly liked them in the western style. Many of these shown here were gifts and are now stored at the Ronald Reagan Presidential Library.

HIS VALUES "The image of the president dressed in cowboy hat and boots at his rugged Ranch in the Sky projected the values of freedom and individualism which his administration advocated."

—Adriana Bosch, television producer and author

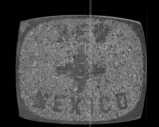

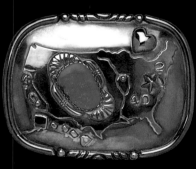

The first lady gives her husband a kiss shortly before his scheduled prostate surgery in early January 1987. Despite protests from his wife and doctors, Reagan went back to work early, giving his annual state of the union address just three weeks after his operation.

HIS VALUES *"Because Ronnie really believes what his mother taught him, that everything happens for a purpose, he doesn't let setbacks or disappointments get him down. If he worries, you'd never know it. If he's anxious, he keeps it to himself. Depressed? He doesn't know the meaning of the word. He's really as relaxed and*

GRACE IN ADVERSITY

On a muggy Friday in July 1985, the Reagans were looking forward to a weekend at Camp David. A medical procedure was scheduled first—the removal of a small, benign polyp from the president's colon—but they did not expect it to interrupt their plans. He had had it done once before; it was nothing major.

After the procedure, Reagan was upbeat and joking as usual, but Nancy Reagan noticed the doctors were not laughing. Privately, they told her they had found a lump the size of a golf ball in his colon. It was probably malignant. There was some concern that the cancer might have spread. Without mentioning cancer, Nancy told her husband that there was a suspicious mass and that surgery was necessary. They decided to have it done the next day.

The operation proved extensive but it went smoothly, and the prognosis was excellent. The large mass had been malignant, but there had been no spread to surrounding tissue.

Reagan was well on his way to recovery when, ten days later, physicians found a small lump on his nose, a minor form of skin cancer. It was easily removed. Typically, the president was unperturbed by his encounters with cancer. Of his colon cancer he said, "Yes, it was major surgery, but it was a minor situation."

Two years later, in January 1987, he displayed similar confidence and resilience after having prostate surgery, going back to work well before the usual six-week recuperation period. He could not maintain such composure, however, when that same year in October, he learned that doctors had found a lump, probably cancerous, in his wife's breast. Mrs. Reagan decided that if it were cancer, she would have a radical mastectomy rather than less extensive surgery followed by chemotherapy and radiation. She wanted it over with. The biopsy was scheduled ten days hence, "the longest ten days of our lives," Reagan said. Keeping her condition secret from all but some family members and her closest aides, Mrs. Reagan bravely kept up her full schedule, hosting a state dinner and honoring all her public commitments.

When the president was told the day of the surgery that the lump had indeed been malignant and the mastectomy had been done, he wept for his wife. But he was by her side when she awoke, assuring her of his love. And when one day later she insisted on getting to her feet and walking, his arms supported her as she began the road to a full recovery.

Though Reagan was optimistic about his health after doctors removed a cancerous polyp from his colon in July 1985, Nancy worried for him. "It was a painful period for me," she later wrote.

hopeful as he appears. I've almost never heard him complain. If something is bothering Ronnie, he'll rarely mention it. And he never tells anyone, not even me, if he's not feeling well. Ronnie is not impervious to events, but he is very resilient. In difficult times, the people around him, including me—all right, especially me—may become nervous and impatient. Ronnie stays calm, and it usually turns out that he was right." —Nancy Reagan

Supported by her husband's arm, Mrs. Reagan is up and walking the day after her own cancer surgery. At right, friends at the White House welcome her home from Bethesda Hospital.

"This was another one of those instances that reminded me of human limitations: For all the powers of the president of the United States, there are some situations that made me feel helpless and very humble. All I could do was pray—and I did a lot of praying for Nancy during the next few weeks." —Ronald Reagan

A VERY MODEST MAN

One day in the Oval Office, Deputy Chief of Staff Michael Deaver noticed that President Reagan was perspiring. Deaver suggested that Reagan take off his coat, as he had often done in the governor's office in California.

"Oh no," Reagan said. "I could never take my coat off in this office." It was more than a matter of personal style: He venerated the office he held, and he was never unmindful of the honor done him by the American people in putting him there. Possessed of power that few can even imagine, he was not exalted by it but humbled—a fact not lost on his biographers and those who knew him best as president. Along with his humor and unfailing politeness, they would remember his humility.

"Even as leader of the United States and head of the Western Alliance, Reagan remained unfailingly modest," wrote biographer Dinesh D'Souza. "Reagan often began public remarks by saying, 'When I got this job . . . ' Of the White House he frequently observed, recalling his childhood,

IT CAN BE DONE

THERE IS NO LIMIT TO WHAT A MAN CAN DO OR WHERE HE CAN GO IF HE DOESN'T MIND WHO GETS THE CREDIT

The president was fond of upbeat mottoes. These two sat on his desk in the Oval Office.

'I'm back living above the store again.' To a group of visitors touring the residence he would say, 'Welcome here to your house, which you're letting me live in for a while.'"

"I think the average American could . . . feel this man was real," Edwin J. Feulner, Jr., president of the Heritage Foundation, once observed. "He was like their father or their neighbor. He shared the same visions, the same concerns. It wasn't an act he was putting on. It was him."

As those who knew him noted, Reagan's genuine humility was not to be confused with meekness or a lack of self-worth. On the contrary, it sprang from a quiet confidence that was nearly unshakable. Reagan's secretary of defense, Caspar Weinberger, noted, "He was a happy man, secure and serene. He knew who he was and he didn't have to impress anybody or try to be somebody he wasn't." For most of his adult life Reagan had been successful, wealthy, and famous. He did not need the presidency for those things; the office did not define him. For that reason, perhaps, he was always aware of the unique privilege of it— and the awesome obligation it entailed.

"Every once in a while I pinch myself sitting opposite the head of state of one or the other of the dozen nations we've visited, thinking this can't be 'Dutch' Reagan here. I should still be out on the dock at Lowell Park." —Ronald Reagan

"The countless Americans I escorted into the Oval Office . . . shared two things in common. They were very nervous before meeting the president. And they were all immediately put at ease by his warm humor and his genuine modesty." —Elizabeth Dole, secretary of transportation and president of the American Red Cross

President Reagan salutes a female Air Force Academy graduate. As commander in chief of the military, Reagan didn't need to defer to anyone—but he valued the men and women who fought for his beloved country. To him, saluting was a necessary sign of respect.

Nancy Reagan cuts the cake at her western-style birthday celebration, surrounded by the president and their friends at the California ranch.

The president's seventy-fifth birthday bash in 1986 was more formal, with close friends joining the first couple at the White House. Celebrating with the Reagans, from left to right, are Walter and Lee Annenberg, Earle and Marion Jorgensen, William and Betty Wilson, and Armand and Harriet Deutsch.

HIS VALUES "The minute he became president, I called him, 'Mr. President.' And he said to me, 'Wait a minute. What's this?' I said, 'Well, you are. And that will be forevermore now.' And he said, 'Not with you, my friend. Not with Earle. Not with my good friends.' I said, 'Well, I will say this: Around anybody, it'll be Mr. President. When we're just a few of us longtime friends, OK, it'll be Ronnie.'" —Marion Jorgensen, family friend

Veteran actors Andy Devine, Walter
Brennan, Buddy Ebson, and Don Defoe
enjoy a light moment with the Reagans
at the Malibu ranch, left, in 1966.
The photo is by Harry Benson. Above,
pal Frank Sinatra joins in celebrating
Reagan's birthday in 1971. Bob Hope
is on Mrs. Reagan's left.

The White House Christmas tree
provides a festive backdrop for the
family snapshot at the far left. At left,
the president talks with Margaret
Thatcher during her visit to Washington
in 1987. They were friends before either
was head of state, and they remained
close after both left office.

President Reagan pays tribute to his wife at a luncheon hosted by the 1988 Republican National Convention in New Orleans, honoring the first lady.

"There was always an air of modesty about him; if you didn't know who he was, you would not know he was the president."

—Shimon Peres, prime minister of Israel

"*Before he was elected, Ronnie had always regarded the presidency with awe. But when he became president, he had trouble believing that other people could be in awe of him. He never looked at it in terms of 'I am president.' Instead, he would refer to the presidency as 'the office I now hold' or even 'this job.' This was genuine. For Ronnie, it would have been presumptuous to view his job in any other way.*" —Nancy Reagan

"When I get together with other political reporters who have been around since the 1960s, we talk some about Kennedy and Goldwater, but it is still Ronald Reagan we talk about most. He is the center, the force. Kennedy is in a special niche ... but Reagan is the most dynamic president I have seen."

—Sam Donaldson, White House correspondent, *ABC News*

The Ronald Reagan Presidential Foundation estimates that the Reagans, either separately or together, have appeared on more than 1,000 magazine covers. Between 400 and 500 are displayed at the Ronald Reagan Presidential Library.

Modern Screen, October 1944

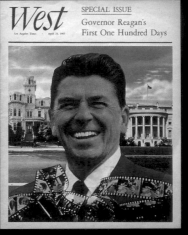

West, Los Angeles Times special issue, April 23, 1967

Newsweek, May 22, 1967

People, February 23, 1976

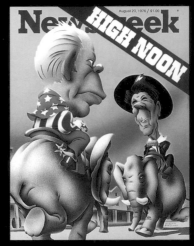

Newsweek, August 23, 1976

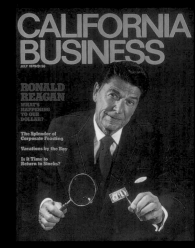

California Business, 1979

New York, July 28, 1980

Esquire, August 1980

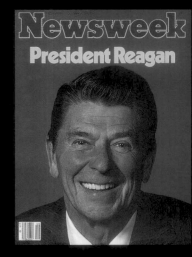

Newsweek, November 17, 1980

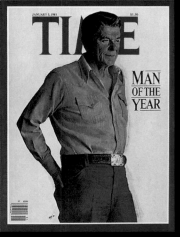
Time, January 5, 1981

The Saturday Evening Post, April 1981

Life, May 1981

Life, October 1983

California, August 1984

Time, January 14, 1985

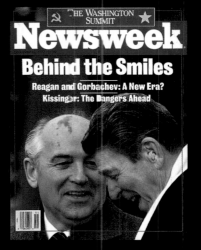
Newsweek, December 21, 1987

Soviet Life, February 1989

People, February 20, 1989

Vanity Fair, July 1998

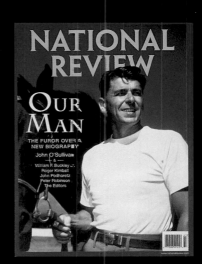
National Review, October 25, 1999

HIS VALUES "There is no doubt that Ronald Reagan had been an actor. And he certainly was a great politician. But he never mistook the Oval Office for the stage; he knew when it was time to act and when it was time to be real. His resolve, dedication, sincerity, and humor, his unending optimism and, above all, simple, devout patriotism and commitment to America's role as a world leader will be forever lasting gifts to his country." —Brent Scowcroft, national security adviser

The president offers a toast to his hostess, Margaret Thatcher, during a trip to London at 10 Downing Street in 1988. Secretary of State George Shultz is on Mrs. Thatcher's left.

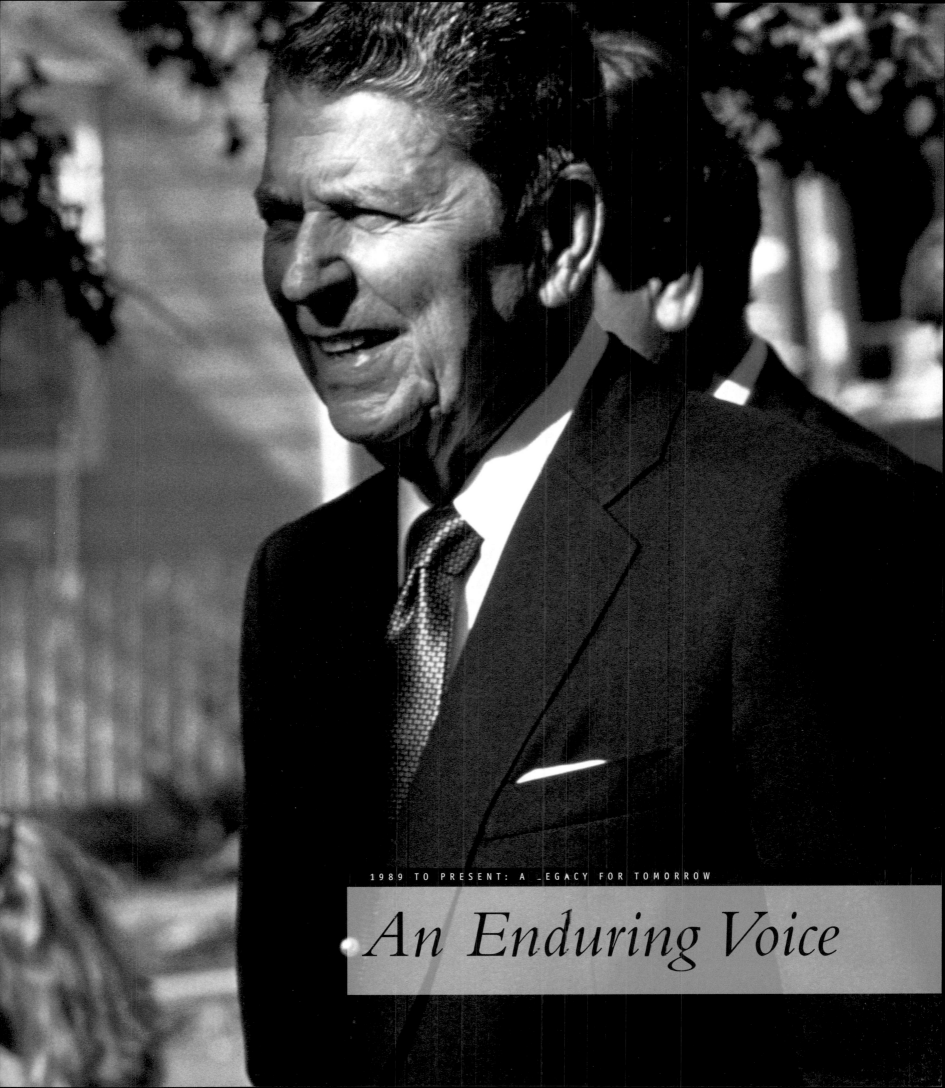

An Enduring Voice

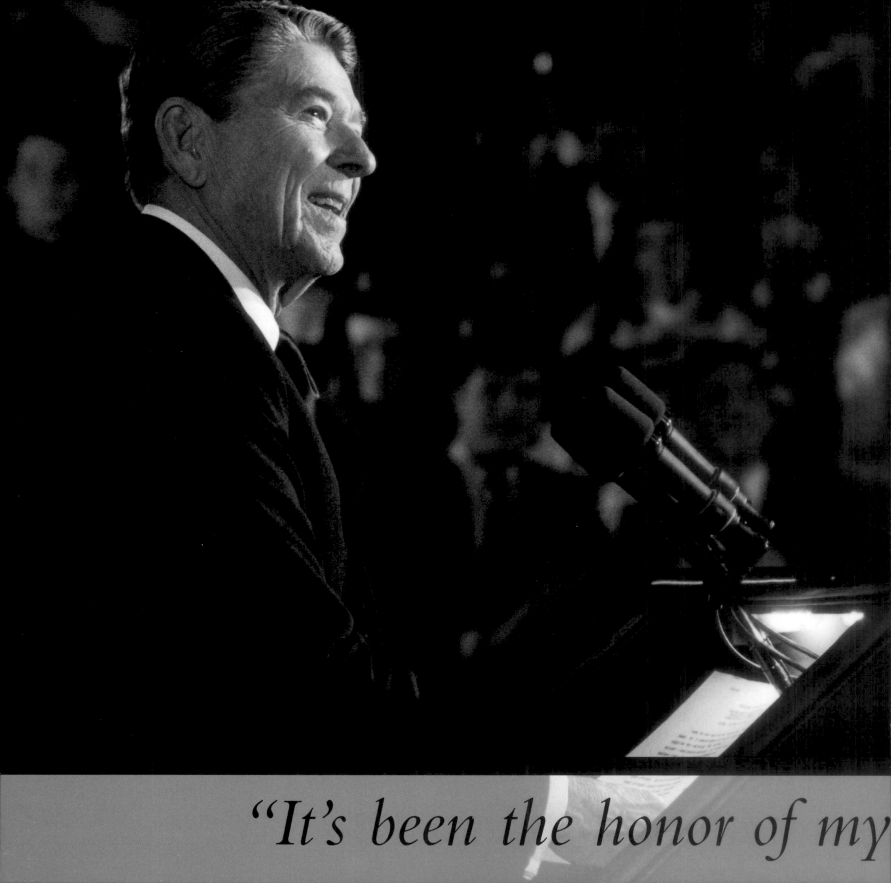

"It's been the honor of my

As his presidency drew to a close, Ronald Reagan could look back on a job extraordinarily well done. When his stewardship began, the country had been directionless and dispirited, its economy in turmoil, its future shadowed by an implacable and well-armed enemy. Eight years later, America was once again proud and prosperous, preeminent in the family of nations, and on the threshold of peace with what had been for decades its most bitter foe. In his farewell speech to the nation in January 1989, Reagan could say with satisfaction that "from Grenada to the Washington and Moscow summits, from the recession of '81 and '82, to expansion that began in late '82 and continues to this day, we've made a difference."

He had also made a difference beyond the borders of the United States. The Berlin Wall was tottering, a metaphor for the collapse of communism in Eastern Europe. On many parts of the globe, totalitarianism and repression were on the defensive and in retreat. As his old friend Margaret Thatcher would say in a 1994 tribute to him, "Ronald Reagan won the Cold War single-handedly, without firing a shot." Thatcher neatly summed up her ally's importance to his nation and the world. "In a time of politicians," she said, "you proved yourself a statesman."

The Reagans had great achievements to look back on, but they also had much to look forward to as they left Washington. After George Bush's inauguration on

life to be your president."

January 20, 1989, they flew to Los Angeles to make their home in Bel Air. There the former president would still be a force in public affairs, working on newspaper articles and finishing his second autobiography. As always, he would be a sought-after speaker, and his speeches would dwell less on goals accomplished than on jobs left undone: a balanced national budget and reduced federal deficit, for instance, and the institution of a line-item veto to allow a president real clout in curbing congressional spending.

Reagan also took an active interest in the Ronald Reagan Presidential Library and Museum in Simi Valley, California. He and four other former presidents were on hand for the 1991 dedication of the hilltop facility, the largest gathering of presidents and presidential families ever assembled. In a tribute to his one-time political adversary, Jimmy Carter said, "Under President Reagan, our nation stood strong and resolute and made possible the beginning of the end of the Cold War. This has led to a new opportunity for our country, to exhibit its greatness which we accept for granted too often, more clearly to people around the world."

Despite their busy schedule on the home front, the Reagans traveled extensively abroad in the early years of his retirement. They visited Germany, Poland, and Russia, where the former president was hailed as a liberator and hero. And of course, there were the getaway jaunts to Rancho del Cielo, the place he and Nancy loved most on earth. In the spring of 1992, an old friend visited them there: Mikhail Gorbachev, out of power in Russia after presiding over the Soviet empire's demise. Gorbachev was pleased with his gift of a cowboy hat but somewhat surprised at the Reagans' little adobe ranch house. It was far less grand than he had expected from such prominent capitalists.

Ronald Reagan made his last visit to his beloved ranch in 1995, and two years later the family sold the retreat to the Young America's Foundation, a nonprofit group that preserves it as it was when he and Nancy lived there. For the Reagans, sadly, it was no longer of much use. Late in 1994, the former president had written a letter to inform shocked and grieving Americans that he was in the early stages of Alzheimer's disease, a progressive, incurable, memory-destroying illness.

With his beloved wife at his side, as always, President Reagan retired, leaving Americans to ponder the accomplishments of his life and what he had bequeathed to them.

"In a president, character is everything. You can't buy courage and decency, you can't rent a strong moral sense. A president must bring those things with him. . . . He needs to have a vision of the future he wishes to create. But a vision is worth little if a president doesn't have the character—the courage and heart—to see it through. Reagan had the vision. Did he have the courage? Yes. At the core of Reagan's character was courage . . . a courage that was ultimately contagious. When people say President Reagan brought back our spirit and our sense of optimism, I think what they are saying in part is, the whole country caught his courage." —Peggy Noonan, author and Reagan speechwriter

On December 9, 1988, Ronald Reagan holds the final press conference of his presidency. He had his differences with some reporters over the years—as every president does—but he said, "I personally liked most of the men and women who covered the White House."

The Reagans wave good-bye at Andrews Air Force Base as they embark for California after Bush's inauguration. "There were warm handshakes, tearful embraces, and lots of picture-taking," Reagan said.

"Following George Bush's inauguration as president, the helicopter carrying the Reagans lifted off from the east front of the Capitol. There were six or seven of us aboard. The helicopter took what has become a ceremonial

HAIL AND FAREWELL

On the evening of January 11, 1989, Ronald Wilson Reagan gave his thirty-fourth and last address from the Oval Office: his valedictory to the nation.

He spoke of his gratitude for the honor of serving as president, of his sorrow at leaving, and of his anticipation of the pleasures of being a private citizen again in his beloved California. Mostly, however, he talked of the pride he felt in America's progress during the 1980s. "It's been quite a journey this decade," he said, "and we held together through some stormy seas. And at the end, together, we are reaching our destination.

"The way I see it," he continued, "there were two great triumphs, two things that I'm proudest of. One is the economic recovery, in which the people of America created—and filled—19 million new jobs. The other is the recovery of our morale. America is respected again in the world and looked to for leadership."

With characteristic modesty, the president credited the people, not himself, for the achievements of his term. He had come to be called the Great Communicator, he said, but the importance of his message had been a matter of content, not style, and the content came from America itself: "I wasn't a great communicator, but I communicated great things, and they didn't spring full bloom from my brow, they came from the heart of a great nation—from our experience, our wisdom, and our belief in the principles that have guided us for two centuries. They called it the Reagan revolution. Well, I'll accept that, but for me it always seemed more like the great rediscovery, a rediscovery of our values and our common sense."

It was common sense, he said, that dictated his policies on tax reduction, free trade, and rebuilding the military—policies that had resulted in a booming economy and a freer, safer world. "As long as we remember our first principles and believe in ourselves, the future will always be ours," he said. "Once you begin a great movement, there's no telling where it will end. We meant to change a nation, and instead, we changed a world."

He called on Americans to nurture and preserve the resurgent national pride of the 1980s and to strive for an "informed patriotism" rooted in "thoughtfulness and knowledge." Finally, he spoke confidently on his presidency, on the Reagan revolution, and on "the men and women across America who for eight years did the work that brought America back.

"All in all," he said, "not bad, not bad at all."

Ronald Reagan leaves the White House for the last time as president. "We were familiar with every room and hallway and had the warmest memories of our life in that beautiful, historic mansion," he said.

swing around Washington for each departing president. As it circled the White House, Reagan looked out the window. He took Nancy's hand and said, 'Look, dear, there's our little bungalow.' Nancy had a tear in her eye; we all did." —Kenneth Duberstein, president's chief of staff

LEGACY

In the eight years he served, President Reagan made the United States the sole superpower on the globe, economically, militarily, and politically. His policies and leadership defeated the Soviet empire, ended the Cold War, and engendered one of the longest periods of prosperity in the nation's history.

Those triumphs alone were sufficient to place him on the shortlist of America's greatest presidents, but along with the concrete achievements, Ronald Reagan left a bequest of the spirit that was equally important: a vision for America and a paradigm for the American character. The vision he famously called a "shining city on a hill," a place not just of prosperity and might but of generosity, inclusion, and simple goodness. It was a city built on the bedrock values that he felt most Americans shared: decency, loyalty, fairness, freedom. It called on what was best in people, appealing not to their fears but their dreams.

He had faith in the American people, and he gave them faith in themselves. He believed that despite human frailty, the instinct for good, when nurtured and encouraged, will result. And his optimism was infectious. Reminded of all they had accomplished and endured, Americans remembered again the unique privilege of being Americans, of being part of history's finest experiment in democracy. Reagan made them proud again, not just of America's wealth and power but of its steadfast stand for what is right and good.

"He was a visionary, a crusader, a prophet in his time," said George Bush. "He embodied the American character." Certainly, he embodied what was best in it. Reagan sought the presidency not for power or personal glory but to serve. He was a unifying force, overwhelmingly elected twice with the support of many Democrats as well as Republicans. He was tough on issues, but did not attack or malign his political opponents. He brought civility, dignity, and grace to public discourse—and to the presidency itself. He also brought courage. Sometimes on the unpopular side of issues, he governed not by polls but according to his own moral compass, looking not for instant acclaim but for the long-range good of his country. He was, he admitted, an old-fashioned man, and his tenure in office resurrected and redefined an old-fashioned word: honor.

Historians would debate whether Reagan had a true political heir, someone as capable as he of leading and of inspiring others to follow. Thus far, most have concluded that he did not. Great leaders are rare.

Reagan received the Presidential Medal of Freedom from George Bush in 1993. It is the United States' highest civil award.

HIS VALUES "His emphasis on moral and spiritual values was one of his greatest contributions. Mr. Reagan made Americans feel good about themselves, no matter what the problems were. More than that, he pointed them to the moral and spiritual foundations which have made this nation great." —Billy Graham, evangelist

"President Reagan's legacy to the world is freedom. His strength of character and bedrock belief in right and wrong ended the Cold War, and his leadership unshackled the yoke of tyranny for millions who had known only oppression."

—Elizabeth Dole, secretary of transportation and president of the American Red Cross

Former president Reagan bestows the first Ronald Reagan Presidential Freedom Award on Mikhail Gorbachev in ceremonies at the Ronald Reagan Presidential Library on May 4, 1992. About a year earlier, Gorbachev had been ousted from power in the Soviet Union by a coup, a prelude to the USSR's dissolution.

Once again enjoying the warmth of Southern California, Ronald Reagan leans against the balcony at the Century Plaza Hotel. Photo is courtesy of Harry Benson.

The Reagans reminisce as they view his portrait in the White House on January 13, 1993. President Bush had just awarded Reagan the Presidential Medal of Freedom, making Reagan the only president to receive the prestigious award in his lifetime. "I consider him my friend and mentor," said Bush of his successor. "And he's also a true American hero."

A LASTING LEGACY

"President Reagan's message was a simple one. It was sometimes seen as naive, simplistic, and lacking in sophistication. It had the sole redeeming virtue of being right. And the world is a better place for his having been right." —Colin Powell, chairman of the Joint Chiefs of Staff

During a celebration at the Ronald Reagan Presidential Library honoring his eighty-second birthday, at left, the former president and Mrs. Reagan receive a pair of silver beakers from Margaret Thatcher. With characteristic optimism, above, Reagan delivers a moving speech at the Republican National Convention in August 1992, his farewell to the party. Checking his watch, he declared that it was, once again, "a time for choosing," encouraging citizens to vote for Bush. Those watching would remember this speech as one of his best.

"Whether we agree with him or not, Ronald Reagan was an effective president. He stood for a set of ideas . . . he meant them, and he wrote most of them not only into public law but into national consciousness." —Edward Kennedy, senator of Massachusetts

HIS VISION "He believed in the simple things. He believed in freedom and democracy. He believed that America was on the right side of history, standing with the forces of good against the forces of evil in the world. And some have dismissed him therefore as an ideologue. But

Ronald Reagan has been justified by what has happened. History has justified his leadership and those strong beliefs." —Richard Nixon, U.S. president

Ronald Reagan enthusiastically endorses George Bush as the Republican presidential nominee at the president's reception dinner in Washington, D.C., 1988.

THE RONALD REAGAN PRESIDENTIAL LIBRARY

Northwest of Los Angeles, on a hill overlooking the Pacific Ocean, stands the Ronald Reagan Presidential Library and Museum, the main repository of the president's legacy. The library was dedicated on November 4, 1991, in ceremonies attended by America's five living presidents at the time: Richard Nixon, Gerald Ford, Jimmy Carter, George Bush, and Ronald Reagan himself.

Built with private funds raised by the Ronald Reagan Presidential Foundation, the library is situated on a one-hundred-acre tract in Simi Valley. The sprawling Spanish-style structure is built around a courtyard, its walls enclosing 153,000 square feet of space. The two floors above ground house a museum, museum store, and the foundation offices. Below ground are two levels where presidential documents and gifts are stored. The library's enormous archives include more than 55 million pages of government records and personal papers, more than 1.5 million photographs, some 769,000 feet of movie film, and more than 100,000 gifts given to the Reagans.

The Reagan Library, however, is more than the sum of its space and artifacts. Its mission is to promote the principles that defined the Reagan presidency—what the Ronald

A large chunk of the Berlin Wall is displayed on the grounds of the Ronald Reagan Presidential Library.

Reagan Presidential Foundation calls Ronald Reagan's Four Pillars of Freedom: individual liberty, economic opportunity, global democracy, and national pride. To that end, the library's public policy arm, the Reagan Center for Public Affairs, has hosted speakers from among the world's great political and moral leaders, among them Margaret Thatcher, Mikhail Gorbachev, Colin Powell, and the Reverend Billy Graham. These and other political luminaries, scholars, and business leaders have spoken at the library about the Reagan legacy and its continuing relevance.

A monument to the past, the library is also intended as a guidepost for the future. On November 9, 1999—the tenth anniversary of the fall of the Berlin Wall—the Presidential Learning Center was founded. Its purpose is "to shape a child's life so that he or she can ably assume the mantle of leadership and help carry forward in the tradition of our Founding Fathers."

For Nancy Reagan, who has devoted much time and energy to the library and its work, it is the young who matter most. "When I see children walking through these galleries," she said, "I'm reassured to know they will learn about my husband's important work." It is they, she pointed out, who will carry on his legacy in the years to come.

"The doors of this library are open now and all are welcome. The judgment of history is left to you, the people. I have no fears of that, for we have done our best. And so I say, come and learn from it."

—Ronald Reagan, in remarks at the opening of the Ronald Reagan Presidential Library and Museum, November 4, 1991

Dedicated to preserving Reagan's legacy, the Ronald Reagan Presidential Library and Museum welcomes close to two hundred thousand visitors a year. Its archives are the largest of any of the presidential libraries.

Since leaving office, our top priority has been to see that Ronnie's achievements can be celebrated forever at the Ronald Reagan Presidential Library and Museum. His modest hope is that it will bear witness to

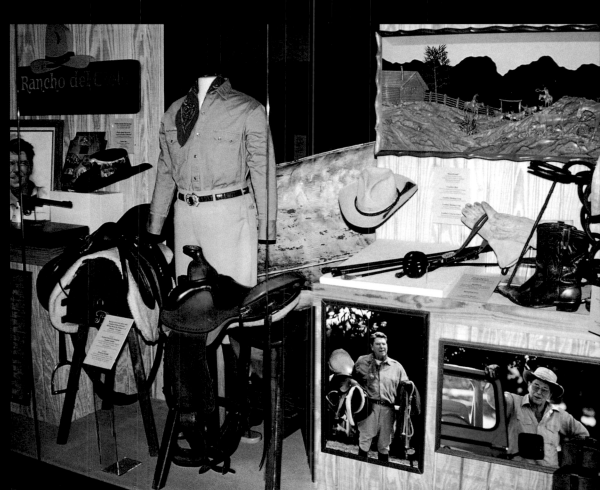

America's five living presidents at the time—George Bush, Ronald Reagan, Jimmy Carter, Gerald Ford, and Richard Nixon— gather at the opening of the Reagan Library. "I guess you and I have run against each other at least once," Reagan quipped to them before the ceremonies.

HIS VISION "Every president makes headlines. It goes with the job. But only a few make history of the kind that affects who we are and how we see ourselves. Ronald Reagan was such a leader. In reviving American confidence, he restored our faith in the presidency itself. The

enormity of his achievements at home and abroad becomes more apparent with every passing year. And as our recognition of this grows, so does our gratitude. I count it a privilege to have shared, even a little, in Ronald Reagan's American journey." —Gerald Ford, U.S. president

With tenderness, the Reagans clasp hands in 1998. The picture, taken by Harry Benson at their home in Bel Air, was one of a few published of the former president as his illness progressed.

HIS VALUES "The longer I live, and the more deeply I delve into the actions, words, and thoughts of Ronald Reagan, the more I treasure them. I am in awe of this great man." —Michael Reagan, son

INTO THE SUNSET

The Reagans left Washington looking forward to a happy, active retirement, and for a while they had it. There was more time for the family and for each other, time for the former president to make speeches and to write. He finished a second autobiography in 1990 and in November 1991 presided over the dedication of the Reagan Library. He turned eighty-one the next February, celebrating in Los Angeles at a gala black-tie fund-raising dinner for the library. Two years later, at another birthday celebration, he spoke in Washington.

It was his last public speech. On November 5, 1994, he shared with millions who loved and revered him the heartbreaking news: During his annual checkup three months earlier at the Mayo Clinic, he had been diagnosed with Alzheimer's disease. It was the same progressive, degenerative, incurable, mind-destroying illness that had killed his beloved mother; Nelle had died of it in 1962. The former president faced it with customary valor and optimism, revealing his illness in a handwritten letter that conveyed his hope that public disclosure might help others.

The president and first lady share a serene moment at Rancho del Cielo in 1981, their "ranch in the sky."

Throughout America and the world came an outpouring of grief, sympathy, and tribute, from the great and the humble, from millions of admirers and from former political foes alike.

"I salute President Reagan for his courage and sharing this private matter with the American people," said his successor, former president George Bush. In Oakland, California, President Bill Clinton departed from his speech at a political rally to tell the crowd: "A few minutes ago, President Reagan announced he was suffering from Alzheimer's disease. And when he said it, it touched my heart in a particular way." He asked the crowd of some four thousand Democrats to join him in wishing the former president well, and in shocked silence they did.

Most who read or heard his final letter were probably most touched by a poignant sentence toward its end. With Nancy beside him, he began, as he said, "the journey that will lead me into the sunset of my life."

Alzheimer's marked the end of Ronald Reagan's uniquely distinguished career. The twilight of a life, perhaps, but the dawn of a magnificent legacy.

"Among all the public figures that I have known in my life none were greater than Ronald Reagan and very few of them measured up to him. He had a basic decency that was wholesomely impressive. The many pictures of this great leader in both of my homes are constant reminders of his fundamental goodness." —Walter H. Annenberg, family friend, philanthropist, ambassador to Spain

At right is the president's handwritten letter to the nation announcing that he has Alzheimer's disease.

"It was the bravest thing he could have done. He's always been my hero, but never more so than when he wrote that letter."

—Maureen Reagan, daughter

RONALD REAGAN

Nov. 5, 1994

My Fellow Americans,

I have recently been told that I am one of the millions of Americans who will be afflicted with Alzheimer's Disease.

Upon learning this news, Nancy & I had to decide whether as private citizens we would keep this a private matter or whether we would make this news known in a public way.

In the past Nancy suffered from breast cancer and I had my cancer surgeries. We found through our open disclosures we were able to raise public awareness. We were happy that as a result many more people underwent testing. They were treated in early stages and able to return to normal, healthy lives.

So now, we feel it is important to share it with you. In opening our hearts, we hope this might promote greater awareness of this condition. Perhaps it will encourage a clearer understanding of the individuals and families who are affected by it.

At the moment I feel just fine. I intend to live the remainder of the years God gives me on this earth doing the things I have always done. I will continue to share life's journey with my beloved Nancy and my family. I plan to enjoy the great outdoors and stay in touch with my friends and supporters.

HIS VALUES "For over half a century, as an actor, politician and president, Ronald Reagan has been a central figure in American life. The dignity with which he accepted the reality of this in hopes that it 'will encourage a clearer understanding of the individuals and families who are affected

Unfortunately, as Alzheimer's Disease progresses, the family often bears a heavy burden. I only wish there was some way I could spare Nancy from this painful experience. When the time comes I am confident that with your help she will face it with faith and courage.

In closing let me thank you, the American people for giving me the great honor of allowing me to serve as your President. When the Lord calls me home, whenever that may be, I will leave with the greatest love for this country of ours and eternal optimism for its future.

I now begin the journey that will lead me into the sunset of my life. I know that for America there will always be a a bright dawn ahead.

Thank you my friends. May God always bless you.

Sincerely,
Ronald Reagan

The Reagans share a tender kiss during his eighty-nineth birthday celebration at their Bel Air home in February 2000.

t' demonstrates how personal tragedy can be converted into a positive force. As Ronald gan has reminded us, great tragedy can spur great good." —David Broder of the *Washington Post*

HIS VOICE "Whatever else history may say about me when I'm gone, I hope it will record that I appealed to your best hopes, not your worst fears, to your confidence rather than your doubts. My dream is that you will travel the road ahead with liberty's lamp guiding your steps and opportunity's arm steadying your way." —Ronald Reagan

AN EMERGING VOICE
[1911-1932]

- February 6, 1911: Ronald Wilson Reagan is born in Tampico, Illinois

- June 1914: World War I begins

- December 1917: The United States enters World War I

- November 1918: The United States and the Allied Forces (chiefly Great Britain, France, and Russia) defeat the Central Powers (Germany, Austria-Hungary, and Turkey), ending World War I

- December 6, 1920: The Reagans move to Dixon, Illinois

- June 1928: Ronald "Dutch" Reagan graduates from North Dixon High School

- October 1929: The stock market crashes, beginning the Great Depression

- June 1932: Dutch Reagan graduates from Eureka College

AN ASPIRING VOICE
[1932-1954]

- September 1932: Dutch Reagan breaks into sportscasting

- November 1932: Franklin Delano Roosevelt is elected 32nd president of the United States

- June 1937: Ronald Reagan moves to Hollywood after signing a seven-year contract with Warner Brothers

- September 1939: Great Britain and France declare war on Germany, beginning World War II

- 1939: The Great Depression ends

- 1940: Ronald Reagan appears in *Knute Rockne—All American*

- December 7, 1941: The Japanese bomb Pearl Harbor, and the United States enters World War II

- 1942: Ronald Reagan stars in the acclaimed *Kings Row*

- April 1942: Second Lieutenant Ronald Reagan reports for duty at Fort Mason

- September 2, 1945: Japan formally surrenders to the Allies (chiefly Great Britain, the United States, and the Soviet Union) and the Axis Powers (Germany, Italy, and Japan) are defeated, officially ending World War II

- 1947: Ronald Reagan is elected to his first term as president of the Screen Actors Guild

- 1948-1953: The Cold War begins when the United States and its European allies form NATO and the Soviet Union explodes its first atomic bomb

- March 4, 1952: Ronald Reagan marries Nancy Davis

A VOICE FOR CALIFORNIA
[1954-1980]

- September 1954-62: Ronald Reagan hosts *GE Theater*

- August 1961: The Berlin Wall is constructed, dividing East Germany from West Germany

- 1961: The United States sends support troops to South Vietnam

- November 22, 1963: President John F. Kennedy is assassinated

- October 27, 1964: Ronald Reagan gives his landmark speech, "A Time for Choosing" on behalf of Barry Goldwater, the Republican nominee for president

- 1964: Ronald Reagan stars in his final movie, *The Killers*

- March 1965: President Lyndon Johnson escalates America's involvement in the Vietnam War

- 1966: Ronald Reagan is elected governor of California

- 1968-1969: Governor Ronald Reagan brings in the National Guard to quell antiwar riots at the University of California at Berkeley

- 1970: Ronald Reagan is reelected governor of California

- 1973: The United States pulls out of the Vietnam War after an unsuccessful struggle

- August 1974: President Richard Nixon resigns in disgrace after the two-year Watergate investigation reveals his part in the scandal

- 1976: Ronald Reagan narrowly loses the Republican nomination for president to incumbent Gerald Ford

- November 4, 1980: Ronald Reagan is elected 40th president of the United States

A VOICE FOR AMERICA
[1981-1984]

- January 20, 1981: Ronald Reagan is inaugurated

- 1981-1983: President Reagan institutes a historic tax-cut package

- March 30, 1981: President Reagan is the victim of an assassination attempt

- March 1983: President Reagan calls the Soviet Union an "evil empire" in a landmark speech to the National Association of Evangelicals

- March 1983: President Reagan announces his Strategic Defense Initiative, and the Cold War again intensifies as the United States and Soviet Union both begin a weapons buildup

- October 1983: The United States invades Grenada

- November 6, 1984: President Reagan is reelected in a landslide

A VOICE FOR THE WORLD
[1985-1988]

- January 21, 1985: President Reagan gives his second inaugural address

- March 1985: Mikhail Gorbachev is appointed general secretary of the USSR

- July 1985: President Reagan undergoes surgery for colon cancer

- November 1985: President Reagan meets with Mikhail Gorbachev in Geneva, Switzerland, in the first of several peace talks

- January 28, 1986: The space shuttle *Challenger* explodes

- 1986-1987: The Iran-Contra scandal plagues the Reagan administration

- June 12, 1987: President Reagan gives his historic speech at the Berlin Wall, challenging Mikhail Gorbachev to "tear down this wall!"

- October 1987: President Reagan meets with Mikhail Gorbachev in Reykjavik, Iceland, for a peace talk that ends in stalemate

- October 1987: Nancy Reagan undergoes surgery for breast cancer

- December 1987: The United States and the Soviet Union sign the INF treaty in Washington, which eliminated a host of nuclear weapons

- November 1988: Vice President George Bush is elected 41st president of the United States

AN ENDURING VOICE
[1989-PRESENT]

- January 11, 1989: President Reagan gives his farewell address to the nation

- November 9, 1989: The Berlin Wall falls, reuniting Germany

- 1991: The Soviet Union collapses, marking an end to the Cold War

- November 1991: The Ronald Reagan Presidential Library and Museum is dedicated and opens for the public

- November 1994: Ronald Reagan discloses to the American public his battle with Alzheimer's disease

*The mission of the Ronald Reagan Presidential Foundation is
to complete President Reagan's unfinished work and to promote the
timeless principles he championed: individual liberty, economic
opportunity, global democracy, and national pride.*

*These Four Pillars of Freedom guided the president throughout
his years in public service and are at the core of all we do.*

[THE LIBRARY AND MUSEUM]

Located in Simi Valley, California, the library houses more than
55 million pages of government documents and personal papers, and
1.5 million photographs. The museum is home to more than 100,000
artifacts chronicling the life and legacy of America's fortieth president.

[THE CENTER FOR PUBLIC AFFAIRS]

This program conducts a forum of ideas where influential leaders
from government, business, industry, media, and academia speak about
the lessons learned during Ronald Reagan's remarkable presidency.

[THE PRESIDENTIAL LEARNING CENTER]

This facility was founded to inspire schoolchildren to learn about
America's great legacy of presidential leadership.

*The Ronald Reagan Presidential Foundation is a nonprofit organization
that sustains the Ronald Reagan Presidential Library and Museum,
the Center for Public Affairs, and the Presidential Learning Center.*

★   ★   ★

Ronald Reagan Presidential Foundation
40 Presidential Drive
Simi Valley, California 93065
TELEPHONE 805-522-2977 FACSIMILE 805-520-9702
www.reaganfoundation.org

★

[PERMISSIONS]

page 2: © 1981 by *Time* magazine. Reprinted by permission.

pages 5, 6, 102, 123, 128, 129, 130, 140-141, 147, 177, 185, 188, 189, 191, 194-195, 203, 205, 213, 220-221, 232, 238, 248-249: © 1997 by Peter Hannaford. Reprinted by permission of HarperCollins Publishers, Inc.

pages 9, 245: Excerpted from a February 1994 birthday tribute to Ronald Reagan.

pages 10, 138-139, 160-161, 173: Excerpts from *Revolution* © 1988 by Martin Anderson. Reprint by permission of Harcourt, Inc.

pages 13, 165, 168, 211, 232, 253: © 1997 by Dinesh D'Souza. Reprinted with permission of the author and The Free Press, a Division of Simon & Schuster, Inc.

pages 33, 45, 46: Used with permission of the Lee County Historical Society, Dixon, Illinois.

page 41, 51: Reprinted by permission of the *Dixon Telegraph,* Dixon, Illinois.

pages 43, 86: © 1987 by Anne Edwards. Reprinted by permission of HarperCollins Publishers, Inc.

pages 44, 47, 56-57: Used with permission of Bill Shaw, publisher of the *Dixon Telegraph*.

pages 49, 62-63, 72, 190: © 1991 by Lou Cannon. Reprinted by permission of International Creative Management, Inc.

page 55: © January 9, 1989, by *U.S. News and World Report*.

pages 68, 98, 100, 117, 118-119, 122, 145, 206, 219, 226: © 1998 by TV Books, Inc. Reprinted by permission.

page 73: David Blundy and John Barnes, *Sunday Times Weekly Review,* May 4, 1980, © Times Newspapers Limited, London, 2000.

page 74: Reprinted with permission of *Variety,* Inc. © 2000.

page 78: © 1940 by the *New York Times*.

page 79: © 1937 by the *Hollywood Reporter*. Reprinted with permission.

page 82: Conde Nast Publications.

pages 84-85, 87, 91: Used with permission of David Robb.

pages 90, 246-247: © 2000 by Peggy Noonan. Originally published in *Time*. Reprinted by permission of William Morris Agency, Inc. on behalf of the Author.

pages 93, 121, 206, 210, 252, 263: Reprinted by permission of Friedman Fairfax.

pages 101, 107, 234: *Vanity Fair*

pages 114-115, 176, 189: © 1989 by Peggy Noonan. Reprinted by permission of Random House, Inc.

page 127: © 1999 by the *New York Times* Company. Reprinted by permission.

pages 132-133, 212: As quoted in "Conservative of the Century" by Senator John McCain, May 1999.

page 142-143: Credits given to the American Enterprise Institute.

page 144: © 1997 by Billy Graham Evangelistic Association. Reprinted by permission of HarperCollins Publishers, Inc.

pages 146, 233, 240-241, 250, 260-261, 263: © 1998 by the Ronald Reagan Presidential Foundation. Reprinted by permission.

pages 150, 210: Reprinted by permission of *Policy Review*.

pages 164, 174, 175, 217, 236: © 1998 by Deborah Hart Strober and Gerald S. Strober. Excerpts from *Reagan: The Man and His Presidency*. Reprinted by permission of Houghton Mifflin.

page 169: David Broder, "End of a Dream," April 1, 1981. © 2000 the *Washington Post*. Reprinted with permission.

pages 172, 207: © 1993 by Margaret Thatcher. Reprinted by permission of HarperCollins Publishers, Inc.

page 182: *People* magazine, "Romances of the Century: Ronald Reagan and Nancy Davis," February 12, 1996. Reprinted by permission.

page 208: © 1982 by *Foreign Affairs,* distributed by the New York Times Special Features/Syndication Sales.

pages 246, 250, 254-255: Excerpted from a November 1991 tribute to Ronald Reagan at the opening of the Ronald Reagan Library.

page 251: Excerpted from a speech at the Ronald Reagan Library.

p. 262: *The Common Sense of an Uncommon Man* © 1998 by Michael Reagan. Reprinted by permission of Thomas Nelson, Inc., Publishers.

page 264-265: David Broder, "Reagan's Example," November 8, 1994. © 2000 the *Washington Post*. Reprinted with permission.

page 264: Excerpted from a speech for the Alzheimer's Association. Used with permission of Maureen Reagan, board member of the Alzheimer's Association.

All quotes by Ronald Reagan and Nancy Reagan printed with permission of the Ronald Reagan Presidential Foundation.

[PHOTO CREDITS]

Allan Tannenbaum/Corbis Sygma: 252-253

AP/Wide World Photos: 135, 148

Corbis Images: 53, 118, 202, 212

Courtesy of Harry Benson: back cover, 18, 176, 219, 234-235, 252, 262

Courtesy of The George Bush Presidential Library: 252, 254-255

Courtesy of The Lee County Historical Society: 26-27, 31, 33, 34, 35, 36, 40, 42, 42-43, 44, 46, 47, 51, 56-57

Courtesy of the Ronald Reagan Presidential Library: 8-9, 10-11, 12-13, 14, 21, 25, 37, 69, 94, 97, 99, 108-109, 113, 137, 138, 142, 150-151, 151, 152-153, 154-155, 156, 160, 161, 162, 163, 164, 166, 167, 168, 172, 174, 175, 177, 178, 179, 182, 183, 184, 184-185, 185, 189, 190, 190-191, 192, 194-195, 196-197, 198, 203, 204, 206, 207, 208, 209, 210, 210-211, 211, 214, 215, 216, 217, 220-221, 222-223, 224, 225, 228, 229, 230, 231, 234, 235, 236, 240-241, 244, 247, 248, 249, 256, 257, 258-259, 259, 263, 265, 266-267

Courtesy of The Screen Actors Guild: 88, 89, 90, 91, 92, 93

Courtesy Gerald R. Ford Library: 139

Courtesy of the *Dixon Telegraph:* 41, 48, 67

David Hume Kennerly/Corbis Sygma: front cover, 16-17, 138-139, 140-141, 159, 186-187, 188, 201, 211, 233, 237, 260-261, 272

Frank Trapper/Corbis Sygma: 251

Franklin D. Roosevelt Library, Hyde Park, New York: 52, 55

From The Allen W. Griffin Collection: 87

From the Irv Letofsky and Brian Ann Zoccola Collection (ronaldreagan-posters.com): 2-3, 38, 39, 58-59, 60, 63, 71, 72, 73, 74, 75, 76, 77, 78, 79, 80, 81, 82, 83, 84, 84-85, 86, 86-87, 87, 115, 116, 117, 125

Gabi Rona/MPTV: 22

J. L. Atlan/Corbis Sygma: 242-243

MPTV: 28

Nancy Reagan Private Collection: 4-5, 6-7, 32, 43, 46-47, 66, 68-69, 70, 76, 76-77, 85, 98, 99, 100, 101, 102-103, 103, 104, 105, 106-107, 110, 114, 121, 122, 122-123, 123, 124, 126, 127, 128, 129, 130-131, 133, 136, 145, 178, 178-179, 220, 234, 235

Ronald Reagan Presidential Library/ David Friend: 1, 45, 49, 50-51, 51, 54, 65, 78-79, 95, 96, 119, 120, 122, 123, 143, 144, 146, 147, 149, 150, 163, 165, 169, 170, 171, 173, 180, 181, 185, 193, 205, 213, 218, 220, 221, 226, 227, 232, 238, 239, 264, 265

Ronald Reagan Presidential Library/Wendy Sparks: 259

Russ Busby: 250

Sacramento Bee: 132, 134

Tina Gerson/Corbis Sygma: 253

WHO Radio 1040 in Des Moines, IA: 68

TEHABI BOOKS

Tehabi Books designed and produced *Ronald Reagan: An American Hero*, and has conceived and published many award-winning books that are recognized for their strong literary and visual content. Tehabi works with national and international publishers, corporations, institutions, and nonprofit groups to identify, develop, and implement comprehensive publishing programs. The name Tehabi is derived from a Hopi Indian legend and symbolizes the importance of teamwork. Tehabi Books is located in San Diego, California. Visit us on the web at www.tehabi.com

President Chris Capen
Vice President of Development Tom Lewis
Design Director Andy Lewis
Editorial Director Nancy Cash
Senior Art Director Josie Dolby Delker
Editor Betsy Holt
Copy Editor Gail Fink
Proofreader Camille Cloutier
Editorial Consultant Martin Anderson

Special thanks to: Laura Foreman, for her incredible editorial talent and her instrumental role in developing this book; William F. Buckley, Jr., for his enthusiastic support; Irv Letofsky; David Hume Kennerly; Martin Anderson, Annelise Anderson, and Kiron K. Skinner of the Hoover Institution; Bill Shaw and the staff of the *Dixon Telegraph;* Bob Gibler and the staff of the Lee County Historical Society; Leslie Waldvogel of the Ronald Reagan Presidential Foundation for her help in selecting the private collection photographs; and Greg Cummings of the Ronald Reagan Presidential Library for his archival research.

Tehabi Books offers special discounts for bulk purchases for sales promotions or premiums. Specific, large quantity needs can be met with special editions, including personalized covers, excerpts of existing materials, and corporate imprints. For more information, contact Tehabi Books, 4920 Carroll Canyon Road, Suite 200, San Diego, California 92121-1725

Dorling Kindersley

LONDON, NEW YORK, SYDNEY. DELHI, PARIS, MUNICH, and JOHANNESBURG

Publisher Sean Moore
Editorial Director Chuck Wills
Art Director Dirk Kaufman

First American Edition, 2001

2 4 6 8 10 9 7 5 3 1

Published in the United States by
Dorling Kindersley Publishing Inc.
95 Madison Avenue
New York, NY 10016

Library of Congress Cataloging-in-Publication Data
Ronald Reagan: an American hero: his voice, his values, his vision/with reflections by Nancy Reagan.
    p. cm.
    Includes bibliographical references.
    ISBN 1-887656-36-7 (limited edition)—ISBN 0-7894-7992-3 (hardcover)
    1. Reagan, Ronald 2. Reagan, Ronald—Pictorial works.
    3. Presidents—United States—Biography.

E877 .R66 2000
973.927'092—DC21
[B]
                00-066636

The paper used in this publication meets the minimum requirements of the American National Standard for Information Sciences—Permanence of Paper for Printed Library Materials, ANSI Z39.48-1984

Printed and bound in Korea through Dai Nippon Printing Company